Praise for *Daddy On Board*

"Dottie Lamm has the ear of a journalist, the soul of a feminist, and the heart of a grandmother. *Daddy On Board* reminds us all that the revolution still must come from within."

—Diane Carman, *Denver Post* columnist
and mother of a thirty-year-old son
and a twenty-seven-year-old daughter

"As the father of a newborn, it's rare anything breaks through my bleary eyes these days besides the needs of the prettiest little girl ever born. Yet Dottie Lamm's stories of successful partnerships provide keen insight for all parents, even though they do not promise more hours of sleep. An absolute pleasure to read."

—Adam Schrager, reporter for Denver's
9News KUSA-TV and father of a
three-and-a-half-month-old daughter

"As every parent discovers, gender roles are forged in the crucible of the family. Dottie Lamm is one of the all-around wisest women I know. In this book she plays part social worker, part sociologist, and part knowing grandmother as she reveals how new parents are upending the traditional divisions of labor, and thus remaking the world, one family at a time. A must-read!"

—Helen Thorpe, writer, mother, and wife
of Denver mayor John Hickenlooper

"A thoughtful look at how modern couples are dealing with today's new realities as they struggle with old, timeless problems: maintaining a successful marriage and raising children prepared for the future. Dottie Lamm's sensitive observations, based in part on her own experience, contain valuable lessons for all young parents."

—Jim Schroeder, lawyer, former government official, husband of U.S. Congresswoman Pat Schroeder, father, and grandfather of four

"Parenthood is an extremely private affair. Most family interactions are hidden from public view, so we rarely witness the day-to-day struggles of other couples who are raising children. Outwardly, our neighbors and friends appear to have perfect lives, so it's easy to feel overwhelmed by our private family struggles that seem uniquely difficult. *Daddy On Board* provides a glimpse into the lives of ten married couples who generously reveal that they're dealing with exactly the same problems as the rest of us. My wife and I laughed about a few of the stories, because the couples in the book echoed, verbatim, some of the conversations we've had in our own home. Thank you for inspiring us, Dottie!"

—Reggie Rivers, former NFL athlete, sports anchor for Denver's *CBS4* KCNC-TV, and father of a four-year-old boy

SPEAKER'S CORNER

is a provocative new series designed to stimulate, educate, and foster discussion on significant public policy topics. Written by experts in a variety of fields, these brief and engaging books should be read by anyone interested in the trends and issues that shape our society.

More thought-provoking titles
in the Speaker's Corner series

Power of the People
America's New Electricity Choices
  Carol Sue Tombari

Social Security and the Golden Age
An Essay on the New American Demographic
  George McGovern

Stop Global Warming
The Solution Is You!
  Laurie David

TABOR and Direct Democracy
An Essay on the End of the Republic
  Bradley J. Young

Think for Yourself!
An Essay on Cutting through the Babble, the Bias, and the Hype
  Steve Hindes

Two Wands, One Nation
An Essay on Race and Community in America
  Richard D. Lamm

For more information, visit our Web site,
  www.fulcrumbooks.com

Daddy
On Board

Daddy
On Board
Parenting Roles for the 21st Century

Dottie Lamm

Library of Congress Cataloging-in-Publication Data

Lamm, Dottie.
  Daddy on board : parenting roles for the 21st century / Dottie Lamm.
    p. cm.
  ISBN-13: 978-1-55591-631-2 (pbk. : alk. paper)   1.   Parenting--Social aspects. 2. Sexual division of labor. 3. Sex role. 4. Work and family. 5. Interpersonal relationships. I. Title.
  HQ755.8L343 2007
  306.8740973'09045--dc22

                    2007031380

Printed in Canada by Friesens Corporation
0 9 8 7 6 5 4 3 2 1

Editorial: Carolyn Sobczak, Faith Marcovecchio, Shannon Hassan
Cover and interior design: Jack Lenzo

Fulcrum Publishing
4690 Table Mountain Drive, Suite 100
Golden, Colorado 80403
800-992-2908 • 303-277-1623
www.fulcrumbooks.com

Contents

Acknowledgments

This book would not have been possible without the inspiration and assistance of:

Sandy Chapman, president of the Denver branch of the National League of American Pen Women, who dragged me (kicking and screaming) into the challenge of writing the original article on this subject for the April 2006 *The Pen Woman* magazine.

Sam Scinta, publisher of Fulcrum Publishing, and his wife, Kristen Foehner, who expressed immediate enthusiasm for this project and offered ongoing encouragement.

Diane Hartman, my longtime friend and my former editor at *The Denver Post*, who provided professional and invaluable early advice and guidance.

Matt Hammer and Michelle Longosz, along with Susan and Phil Hammer, parents and grandparents, respectively, of Mateo and Mikaela, who have enlightened me with their parental insights and sustained me with their friendship over the years.

The ten couples I interviewed, who gave me the ultimate gift of their time, their enthusiasm, and their willingness to share (along with their tolerance of my never-ending e-mails!).

My grown children and their spouses, Heather Lamm and Alex Ooms, Scott and Cindy Lamm, who have included us in their lives (and "allowed" me to write about them) and the lives of our grandsons, Jasper Lamm Ooms, three, Kennon Hunter Lamm, one, and Tobias Vennard

Ooms, three months.

Psychotherapy and coaching experts Laurie Weiss and Leslie Hilton, who permitted me to pick their brains and quote them freely.

The numerous friends and acquaintances from my own generation, the "middle" generation, and the younger generation who weighed in with humor and pathos about "the way we were" and how we live now.

My editor, Carolyn Sobczak, and the other talented staff at Fulcrum, who went way beyond the call of duty with their energy, their patience, their dedication to this project, and their exacting standards, which kept me on my toes.

Last, but not least, my husband and partner of forty-four years and absolutely super "Granddaddy On Board," Dick Lamm.

Introduction
Coming Full Circle

I've spent the last forty-five years traveling to other worlds. Strong images from these journeys remain deep within me.

For example, there were the pregnant women with up to seven children in tow that Dick and I observed on our 1963 mountain climbing honeymoon to the Peruvian Andes. Most dramatic were their weary but stoic faces as they struggled along the steep, narrow paths, all of them burdened with water buckets filled from the well or bundles of firewood gathered from the forest.

I also recall the sick, thirsty, and sometimes dying refugees from Pol Pot's Cambodia in the camps on the Thai border. Traveling there in 1979 on an official tour when Dick was governor of Colorado, we tried—often with a heartbreaking lack of success—to soothe their raging fevers, hush their children's tears, and offer some glimmer of hope.

Later, as a U.S. delegate to and participant in the 1994 U.N. Conference on Population and Development, in Cairo, and in the 1995 Fourth World Conference on Women, in Beijing, I witnessed the power of women from all walks of life bursting into their own. Beijing was perhaps my happiest foreign journey, from reveling in the pride of Latin American peasant women setting up their own small businesses and showing others how to do it to watching in awe as the burka-covered Muslim women from Yemen entered into negotiations on "women's rights as human rights."

Closer to home, I've also seen other worlds.

In 1964, I became a social worker for families on public assistance at the Denver Department of Human Services, where I tried to help the moms and/or dads get what they needed from the system and then move on to independence. Two years later, while pursuing my master of social work at the University of Denver Graduate School of Social Work, I strove to ease the sadness of single pregnant women at Florence Crittenton Home who, in those days, gave birth to their babies then released them for adoption.

As the first lady of Colorado for twelve years, and then as the Colorado Democratic U.S. Senate candidate in 1998, I visited and took part in the ceremonies and celebrations of African American churches, rural rodeos, Hispanic fiestas, and even, occasionally, all-male clubs as the featured speaker.

Throughout these journeys, I chronicled stories of the disenfranchised as a columnist, publicly promoted policies to improve the lives of women and children as a politician and feminist, and privately tried to walk in the shoes of my clients and patients as a social worker. I concentrated my passion on the journeys of others and on trying to enable their positive outcomes. At the same time, I mostly ignored the issues in my own life and the challenges of fellow "travelers" in my socioeconomic group. In writing this book, I've come home, full circle, to where my more personal journey began.

It was while walking in my own shoes, as a 1970s middle-class married mother with two small children and a budding on-and-off career, when the impact of everything—the push-pull of the home and the workplace, the drastically altered relationship between husband and wife once kids arrive, and the entrenched paternalism in America, rampant then (and still alive today)—hit me full force.

I discovered quickly that just because you are an educated professional, you don't necessarily escape the fear that the child-care provider will not show up, the panic of breast milk letting down when you have just one last thing to finish at work, or the attitude that somehow working mothers are a lesser species. Two examples from 1970 will never leave my memory.

Once, at work, I watched as a white male colleague, a civil rights worker and a professed "liberal," looked straight at a female colleague, a widowed mother of two teenagers, and proclaimed, "Equal pay is necessary for blacks and other minorities, but not for women, as they have husbands to support them."

The second instance hit even closer to home. As my husband's political career was ramping up and our second baby was on the way, I decided to drop my career for a while and stay home as a full-time mother and helpmate. My mother-in-law's comment was "I'm glad you are finally going to stay home and be a *real* mother!"

Added to that was the oft spoken and sometimes unspoken assumption of my husband and others: "Now that you're not working, you can add this, this, that, and that to your day."

Fast-forward thirty-seven years. I am now a grandmother of three boys. I'm a seventy-year-old biking and hiking enthusiast, a breast cancer survivor of twenty-six years, a recovering politician, a semiretired teacher and counselor, and a writer in the process of passing on whatever small bits of hard-won wisdom I have gleaned from all my journeys.

As I watch my grown children and their spouses wrestle with the juggling act of working in their professions and caring for their children, I am amazed. First, I see how much has changed after four decades in how middle-class professional parents operate and negotiate within their marriages, and second, I see how much has not!

Therein lies the subject of this book.

This is not a book on child rearing—Do you follow Spock or spank the child?—but on how couples may come to agreements about who does what, how, when and how much, and how these parenting roles have changed over the years.

This is also a book about the emotional climate surrounding those decisions, the constant tug of tradition that says, "Don't change!" and how men and women learn to change anyway, often from each other.

This is not a book on what you *should* do as a father or a mother, but what you *actually* do—and why. How do you either fall into or negotiate parental roles with your spouse?

Then, how do you come to terms with your own expectations and the expectations of your parents, living or dead? How do you deal with the attitudes of your peers, who are often waiting in the shadows to pounce on any decision you make? For even as adults, we never quite escape the pull of peer pressures lingering on from our teenage years. Thus come the mommy-against-mommy judgments, or the mandate that dads fit the superstrong, alpha male, breadwinner model, even when fathers' own dads didn't push that model on them.

This book is not an academic research project. Only enough statistics will be provided to give context and to highlight differences.

This is also not a policy paper. While I realize that what government, businesses, charitable groups, and religious organizations do can drastically affect the way couples see and negotiate their roles, I'll save that subject for another time. This book will concentrate on personal relationships more than public policy.

Some may call this an elitist work, as I focus on professional-level married couples. Yet these are the people who have the financial means to at least consider a variety of choices.

I interviewed ten married couples who have children ranging in age from four months to seventeen years. In most cases, each individual member of a couple completed and returned a questionnaire before the joint interview. Five of these couples are dual-income professionals. Two are stay-at-home-mom couples. Three are stay-at-home-dad couples.

I have also informally queried dozens of couples and individuals my own age who began child rearing in the late sixties or early seventies; corporate executives, psychotherapists, job coaches, friends; my own children and their spouses; and other couples with small children whom I encounter in everyday life. The one thing all these parents have in common is the emotional investment in their children and the mission to raise good, productive, and creative adults.

Author Calvin Trillin wrote in his book *About Alice* that when he and his late wife discussed the myriad child-rearing theories endlessly promoted by their contemporaries, they came to agree on a simple notion: "Your children are either the center of your life or they're not, and the rest is commentary."

For every one of my couples, their children are clearly the center of their lives. What keeps them at that center through the storms of parental conflicts and the oceans of work and life pressures might be useful information for others in similar, or even different, family boats. This is not to suggest that all the dilemmas can be solved or that they will be solved in the scope of this book. But I, with the help of the new-generation parents I encountered, can take a crack at some of them.

So I venture forward, hoping other parents can enter into this dialogue about parenting roles in the twenty-first century and perhaps find a new solution to a common challenge, or at least identify with some of these couples' stories with an "aha!" moment:

Hey, that's me!

That's us!

So *that's* how they got through it.

Hey—if she or he can do it, so can I.

What?! We never thought of *that*!

Chapter One
The Way We Were

I had not yet read Betty Friedan's breakthrough book, *The Feminine Mystique*, but my husband and I already agreed: *We* were going to do it differently.

It was 1963. Just married and back from our South American honeymoon, we planned the big and little details of our lives as we settled down in Colorado. Yes, we each loved and admired our own mothers, both full-time homemakers. And yes, we would bring our parents' family values to our own marriage and future family. But I would have my own social work career, equal to his law career. Early on, my husband announced, "I will go anywhere, anytime for you to realize your dreams."

We would share household responsibilities. He brewed the morning coffee, put out cereal and toast, then prepared the brown-bag lunches, replete with sandwich, apple, and cookie, for us to take to our respective jobs. I shopped for groceries and cooked dinner. He cleaned up.

We both pitched in on weekends. We packed in the extra chores as we packed up for our numerous ski and mountain climbing trips. Our goal for the house, even when we had dinner or stay-over guests, was to have it presentable, not spotless.

It worked—for four years. *Then*, we had kids! That's when the traditional roles we had known since childhood kicked in with a vengeance.

When our son, Scott, was born in 1967, I switched to

part-time work. After all, I was breast-feeding, so it just made sense. When our daughter, Heather, was born in 1970, I decided to quit my social work job altogether for a while. After all, Dick was earning more money as a lawyer and building up political steam, so it just made sense. Did I begin doing most of the kid stuff and housework? Of course! I was home. It just made sense.

A year or so after Scott was born, my supervisor at work, a psychologist and lay analyst at the University of Colorado Health Sciences Center, said to me, "You would make a talented child analyst. Let me see if I can get you into the training program with Anna Freud. Of course, you would have to go to London. …" When I told Dick about this conversation, he beamed with pride, I swelled up with professional worth—and we both laughed. This happened only five years after his "I would go anywhere" speech, yet neither of us gave this option serious thought. I wasn't even angry about my missed opportunity. His career was becoming supreme; mine was becoming secondary, soon to be nonexistent. We had become our parents.

> It might have been the end of the turbulent sixties and the beginning of the feminist seventies, but most college-educated, middle-class married women still lived under the post–World War II ethic: stay home and tend to your husband and offspring.

It might have been the end of the turbulent sixties and the beginning of the feminist seventies, but most college-educated, middle-class married women still lived under the post–World War II ethic: stay home and tend to your husband and offspring. In 1975, only 47 percent of married women with children of any age were in the workforce, compared to 73 percent in 2000. And for those 1970s college-educated moms with infants or preschoolers, their labor force participation rate was lower than that of any other parent group demographic. By 2004, the percentage of workforce participation by college-educated, married women with children reached 81.8 percent. No wonder this decade of daddies is coming on board!

But back to the way we were.

A woman about my age who had been deeply involved in the anti–Vietnam War and civil rights movement in the sixties said to me recently, "I *knew* that—I knew that if I married him I was marrying not just him, but his *life*—that's why it took me eleven years to decide to marry him at all."

Another couple of the same era, dual-career and hard-driving, tried to be creative. They moved to a commune where child-rearing roles would be shared "equally by all." Quickly disillusioned by the chaotic nature of the place, they moved out. So how did they make it work? "We didn't," quipped the wife with both a smile and an edge to her voice. "The only thing that kept us from divorcing was that we couldn't decide who *wouldn't* get the kids."

One of my sorority sisters who recently visited told me that her husband, a high-powered attorney from the beginning, wouldn't even do the dishes *before* their three children were born. When she complained, he told her that he would work harder and make more money so that she could hire help, but that he would *not* do dishes. Laughing, she admitted that she was part of the problem: "I was antifeminism and basically loved homemaking, so I really bought the whole program."

> "I *knew* that—I knew that if I married him I was marrying not just him, but his *life*—that's why it took me eleven years to decide to marry him at all."

A social work colleague whose husband left early for his high-powered job downtown and came home after their three kids were in bed told me she once confronted him: "Why don't you just get an apartment in town for the week, then come home and *really* be with us on the weekends?!" Did he? "No, but it made me feel better just to get it out."

Recently we had dinner with some longtime political friends. During an intense discussion about how our grown boys and sons-in-law seem to be so involved with their children, the wife commented that her husband couldn't even remember which schools each of their four kids attended. He bristled, "I could too! Still can!" and proceeded to rattle off the names of the schools. He then smiled sheepishly and admitted that his accurate memory did not mean he was really hands-on—not anything like the way his own sons were raising their kids.

One woman, a teacher, came to terms with the fact that her pediatrician husband was never home with their own children by reidentifying herself. "I just decided that I was going to consider myself a married single mother, because that was how it was going to be for a while."

Whatever philosophical means the moms of the sixties and seventies used to get through the parenting years, the same concrete fact remains: These college-educated mothers, whether working outside or inside the home, whether angry, conflicted, or adjusted, did approximately 90 percent of the child care, child nurturing, and child-related activities, although a few women I talked to did say that their husbands were great with the typically male jobs—car maintenance, yard work, and the like. However, I've talked to very few college-educated fathers my age who feel they did more than four to eight hours of child care and/or housework a week, and that time would often include piling the kids in the car to get ice cream or go to the park; in short, the typical daddy fun stuff.

Have times really changed? Are younger dads actually changing diapers, serving up meals, and, more than that, feeling as responsible for what happens on the home front as moms always have?

Well … yes. Sometimes in spoonfuls, sometimes in spades. But yes!

Chapter Two
Daddy On Board!

The mom in her mid-thirties perched on a stool in a downtown Denver restaurant as her daughters, seven months and three years old, bounced on each knee. We were at a 2006 postelection fund-raiser. Her husband, a political consultant, wove his way toward her through the crowd, her drink in hand, and offered to feed the baby.

"Oh, I don't know," shrugged the mom (also a full-time career person). "What time did she last eat?" At which point Dad whipped out his BlackBerry to check.

Click! That's what we old feminists used to say when a new revelation about gender roles suddenly struck. This guy isn't just being nice to his wife or wanting to spend quality time with his infant—he's really been in charge of the kids' schedule all day!

Actually, the concept of "dads on board" inched its way into my consciousness before this 2006 event.

A few years ago, walking in the park on a sun-speckled Saturday with a young female friend, I mused at the sheer number of dads with kids at the playground. When I wondered aloud whether this was due to an increased divorce rate, my friend retorted, "No way—I know a lot of these guys. They're married, and Saturday is their day."

"The *whole* day?" I asked. "Yes," she replied, "and sometimes the whole weekend!"

Hmmm, I thought, thinking back thirty or forty years ago when dads sometimes took the kids for an hour or two's excursion on weekends and called it "babysitting."

Not long after my revelation in the park, both of my kids had children of their own. I was astounded that our daughter Heather's husband, Alex, did 30 to 40 percent of the baby care for infant Jasper, born June 2004, even though Alex was working full-time and Heather was on maternity leave. With the exception of breast-feeding, he was both willing and able to do everything she did, including the diaper changing that our generation of dads had studiously avoided. Often, in the early summer mornings Alex would snuggle Jasper in the soft, chest-hugging baby carrier and head for the park as the family's two gigantic Bernese mountain dogs, Oakley and Argos, bounded ahead.

And our son, Scott; who was able to take time off when he and his wife, Cindy, welcomed Kennon in October of 2006, did close to 50 percent of the feeding, changing, and rocking of Kennon, in addition to most of the schedule planning and errand running. Then, upon returning to work when Kennon was three months old, Scott exhibited some of the same sadness and anxiety typical of new mothers who leave an infant for a job.

Is this the brave new world or what?

Well, yes and no.

The Modern Traditional Family

I interviewed two couples in which Dad was the full-time wage earner and Mom was the full-time homemaker. In each couple, the father had been raised in the same kind of traditional family himself. Yet each felt he wanted to be at least somewhat more hands-on with his children than his own dad had been.

It may look like the same structure, but the content is new.

Public affairs consultant Eric Anderson, forty, and his wife, journalist Renate Robey, forty-four, made the joint decision that she would quit her career and stay home after their first child was born. Sitting at their homey, cluttered dining room table, the surrounding walls colorfully decorated with kids' paintings, Renate talked with an animated voice and hand exclamations as the children, Elliott, six, and Charlotte, three, romped in the living room.

"I'm suited to it. Of course there are those days that are brilliant and beautiful and things are good; then [there are] those days when [the kids] barf all over me. ... But good and bad days happen at paid work too." Renate added that by the time she quit her fifteen-year journalism job, she only liked about 30 percent of it anyway. Financially, both felt that for her to work was a wash, as her paycheck would be consumed by the cost of child care.

By taking care of things at home, Renate could make it easier for her husband to build his business. Each had watched the panic their friends experienced when both parents worked full-time. The same questions always come up: When a child is sick, which parent takes time off from work? How do they decide whose work is more important? Who takes off early to pick a child up from soccer? Who puts a meal on the table?

Eric, hard-charging at work and high-energy at home, spoke eloquently of the sense of "ease and confidence" that allows him to just "walk out the door with peace of mind" because Renate is watching the home front.

"He gives me lots of emotional support," says Renate, which she admits she needs. "He tells me often that he appreciates what I do. He takes an interest in our daily details. He tells others that we've found a formula that works for our family. I love hearing that. I could not, would not, stay home without [that kind of] support!"

Yet Eric's support stretches far beyond the emotional. Despite his fifty-hour-a-week job, he figures he spends twenty-five more hours with the children and on child-related activities, including weekend excursions to the park, "which is loaded with other dads!"

When I say that I have observed that phenomenon, he laughs and adds, "Yeah! It's like the moms have said, 'They're *yours* today ... GO!!'"

"I love reading to the kids the books that were read to me. Decades seem to disappear when I open books like Richard Scarry's Busytown stories and the Babar books," Eric wrote to me in a follow-up e-mail. "I don't think I was prepared for how a parent quickly and profoundly falls in love with children. ... This degree of love, however, brings with it anxiety. What if something were to happen to them? What if my momentary carelessness causes them harm?"

Eric gives this example of putting Elliott on the metal playground merry-go-round when he was a toddler:

> I didn't want it to be a boring ride, but centrifugal force becomes powerful at a certain speed, and he was young. One time I was spinning him a little too fast and I saw him starting to fall off when he was on the opposite side of the merry-go-round from me. I reacted quickly and, fortunately, he didn't completely separate from the merry-go-round until he had spun right in front of me, and I caught him perfectly, knowing that it was pure dumb luck that he didn't fall off at a different point in the cycle. He was a little surprised but perfectly safe. ... And because he was whole and healthy, Renate never needed to know about it! ... [So] I tend to be at a high level of alert when I'm caring for them. But I also am wary of being the 'helicopter' parent whose overprotective hovering results in a child who is fearful and hesitant. You can see how office work would be relaxing in comparison.

This level of anxiety and on-the-job figuring it out is prevalent in some degree in each of the dads I interviewed.

It's not that older-generation dads didn't love their kids and worry about them; they just were not on the front lines nearly as often to make those freedom versus protection split second decisions.

Jon and Stephanie Bender tell a similar tale to Eric and Renate's.

Stephanie, thirty-eight, a former social worker with at-risk teens at Denver's Department of Human Services, loved her job, "especially the kids," but had no qualms about quitting when her second son arrived. She had continued working part-time after her first son was born, as Jon's mother was able to babysit.

It's not that older generation dads didn't love their kids and worry about them; they just were not on the front lines nearly as often to make those freedom versus protection split-second decisions.

"I will eventually go back, but there's not a moment in the day to even think about missing it now!"

Stephanie and Jon, a litigator for Holland & Hart, "relax" in their home, which looks out on a spacious backyard, bright white after a third holiday snowstorm. Now the parents of Teddy, five years old, Kyle, three, and Lucy, five months, they somehow manage to carry on a coherent conversation while the two boys pop in and out and Lucy, slightly fussy, is passed back and forth between them. Both parents, casual in jeans and sweatshirts, good-naturedly bemoan the fact that the prior evening, spent at the home of good friends and their kids, was much fun for all, but "took its toll in terms of sleep."

"Most of our close friends seem to be couples with small children, where the mom stays home," says Stephanie. "And we get together with them as much as we can."

Jon, thirty-five, was allowed two weeks of paternity

leave by his law firm with the birth of each child, but he only took five days when Lucy was born because of competing work demands.

"Yet," says Stephanie, "Jon comes home each night and just steps right in [with the kids]—before even a bite to eat or anything. My mother is beyond impressed with what Jon does."

Jon smiles, and when asked if such dedication is totally exhausting after a full day of litigation, he smiles again.

"It depends," he says. "When work at the office has been energizing, it's easy. When it's depleting, then child stuff is even more depleting."

Even so, Jon, who's very relaxed and laid-back for a lawyer, estimates he does about thirty hours of child-related activities a week.

"I can't imagine not spending this time," says Jon, who listed on his questionnaire "story time at night" and "playtime on weekends" as his favorite kid activities. He tries not to bring work home in the evenings, except in a real emergency. He'd rather stay late at the office, because after he spends "max time" with the children at night, he's too totally worn out to work after they are in bed.

Three common themes stand out with these two stay-at-home-mom families.

1. Age. Both women are older mothers—late thirties or early forties—and neither feels she has to prove herself as a professional or a feminist. Been there, done that.

2. Spousal respect. Both husbands admire and approve of their wives' choices, support them psychologically, and want hands-on involvement with their kids when they are home, despite their own exhaustion.

3. Money. First, both couples are middle-class and financially secure, though often feel stretched. Second, neither husband takes the attitude that "*I* earn, so watch what *you* spend," which is sometimes prevalent in stay-

at-home-mom families. In fact, in the Bender family, Stephanie takes charge of the family finances, and Jon says she is more frugal than he sometimes wants her to be.

With Eric and Renate, who both agree she never has to ask for money or permission to spend, the following dialogue occurred:

Eric: "I think you feel you don't deserve to spend, as you aren't making any money."

Renate: "Not true! I'm just naturally frugal. I can't stand to buy something that's not on sale. Paying full price goes against my grain!" Renate, who revels in her big splurge—a new minivan—still agonizes over the bids they recently received to remodel and enlarge their small house.

"Don't worry," says Eric with an affectionate grin, "we can afford it."

Both admit with some compassion that many couples who have made the choice they have made cannot afford *any* of the extras, and if that were the case for them, the decision for Renate to stay home would be harder.

Also, some women in the "mommy literature" show more ambivalence when they make that decision to stay home full-time, even when they feel it is the right and best thing to do. Miriam Peskowitz, in her 2005 book, *The Truth Behind the Mommy Wars*, writes that after quitting her job as a college professor when her daughter was born, she was besieged by the voices asking, "What have I done?" "My joyful devotion to being home with my daughter did not seem to quiet them, as I'd hoped they might, and this surprised me. The voices were my private Greek chorus."

Peskowitz's ambivalence parallels my own experience years ago, when I quit my job to be a full-time stay-at-home mom. My brain knew I had done the right thing at the right time for both myself and my family—my children would only be toddlers/preschoolers once, and my husband's political career might be short, whereas I could return to my career at any time—but my heart still felt torn between two worlds.

And some slightly older moms (than those in this study) whom I have talked to—especially those who quit high-level positions while their husbands' high-powered careers continued full steam ahead—think their choices were the best for all concerned, but still find themselves feeling somewhat diminished, disempowered, and isolated. One said, "For me, there is no panacea. Emotional and professional balance is a distant dream."

The Twenty-First-Century Norm: Dual Income with Kids
A recent trend much heralded by the media and debated by feminists shows that some professional women are stepping off the career path and becoming full-time home-makers, as Renate and Stephanie have done. Nevertheless, the overwhelming majority of married couples with kids are dual-income parents—75 percent, according to the Census Bureau.

Taking into account that most wives and mothers from working-class families, especially those in minority and recent immigrant groups, have always worked outside the home, the trend for college-educated, professional women to pursue careers after they are married and have children has climbed dramatically. In 1948, only 17 percent of *all* married women were in the workforce. Yet by the year 2005, approximately 75 percent of all married women with children were employed outside the home, and, more per-tinent to this study, almost 63 percent of *college-educated moms with infants* were in the workforce!

This trend has been fed by a number of factors:

1. The exploding cost of housing and the equally daunting future cost of college.

2. The feminist movement, which propelled women to prove themselves through paid work, or at least gave them

permission to fulfill career aspirations and financial goals while at the same time marrying and starting a family.

3. Inflation, which has eaten away at the dollar so that one paycheck doesn't cover what it used to.

4. The simple desire of women to use their professional skills and/or to make their own money for their personal financial security or sense of self-worth.

Whatever the motivation for women (and it's often a combination of factors), the attitude of even the most traditional male has changed radically from "You must stay home because, as a man, I must prove that I alone can support my family"—a view that was still prevalent in the sixties and seventies—to "Let's see what works."

Many modern fathers also have a strong desire to be a different kind of parent, and a much more involved father, than their own fathers were. At least in the dads I interviewed, this desire does not stem from a need to rebel against their dads or from some long held resentment toward their less-involved fathers. In fact, the young dads gave tribute to the "old guys" for doing the best they could at the time. Responses such as the following, more wistful than angry, were typical.

I wish my father was around and involved more when I was growing up. ... I think it was generational. ... My mom was the traditional housewife who met our needs. He did take me to ball games and to his place of work when I was older.

My father, although very kind and loving, had little to do with child rearing. He worked in a factory, came home, had dinner, and dozed in his chair. My family was work-ing-class and both parents loved [us] kids, but they were very traditional.

My father seemed to have time even though he was the working provider. He was passionate about family time … yet I hope to be more emotionally available [to my kids].

However, after giving their dads their due, the fathers in my sample passionately wanted to be different. It was not just a matter of "helping my wife" or "doing my share." It was a real recognition of the emotional rewards, for themselves and their kids, of being a hands-on dad from the beginning.

> "I could not imagine being—or want to be—less involved in my children's growth and care. I can't imagine not being a hands-on father."
> —Rob Carmody

Rob Carmody states this priority eloquently: "I could not imagine being—or want to be—less involved in my children's growth and care. I can't imagine not being a hands-on father."

And Rob was hands-on from the beginning. In an e-mail following our interview, he writes the following about the birth of his first daughter, Mattie Marie, now three, who was born by cesarean section: "I asked the nurse if I could touch her. She said, 'Of course you can, you're her daddy.' She was so tiny (5 pounds, 4 ounces). I stuck one finger out and touched her leg and at that point I realized I was a daddy and the warmth of elation filled me up." And about the second twelve weeks of Mattie Marie's life, when Rob took parental leave, he says:

I learned by observation how to see the signs for feeding, sleeping, and the need for a clean diaper. … I am very routine driven and once the baby and I got on the same page, it was very easy for me to anticipate and plan our day. I knew when she would be tired, hungry, and need a diaper change. I planned our activities around naps, took long walks and had time to make meals, do laundry and search for our future nanny. It was quite a role reversal from what most people get to experience. ... Mattie and I bonded very closely and I feel that this has had a lasting effect on her as the two of us get along great together three and a half years later.

Rob's family leave—from his job as a geographic information systems specialist for the City of Aurora—was unpaid. At the time of this interview, he was on a second unpaid leave to care for daughter Mackenzie, born in late June 2006, and feels fortunate that he has been financially able to do this. He took each leave after his wife's twelve-week paid maternity leave was up, so that the girls would have six months of "steady parent time."

The girls' mom, Kim Ashley Carmody, thirty-five, is a director for the MediaNews Group in downtown Denver. At the time of this interview at the end of 2006, Kim had been back at work full-time, from her home basement office, since late September. While Rob cares for Mackenzie, a nanny comes in on weekdays to care for and transport Mattie Marie, who has just started preschool.

Their comfortable home, a three-bedroom ranch, which they have largely remodeled and decorated themselves (replete with hand-painted murals in the girls' bedrooms), seems amenable to this lively gang of five. But today Rob and Kim are low-key. It's almost the New Year, the weather is cold, and snow covers their yard. They appear tired, but lighten up with new energy when Mattie Marie pops into the room, blond curls bouncing.

One of their current struggles revolves around whether they should move. They love the racial and religious diversity of the area. An archconservative African American church, a synagogue, and a multiracial church with a gay and straight congregation are almost within view of their home. And they especially appreciate the area's proximity to both of their workplaces. Each groans at the thought of moving to the suburbs. Then they laugh, admitting that "better schools and the prospect of a larger home for the same amount of money" is appealing. Again, in unison, they groan about the 'burbs, and Rob rolls his eyes in partial mock distress.

Turning serious, Rob and Kim voice their real concern about the crime in their area. Last summer there was a drug-related shooting at a house in the same corner position as theirs on the block behind them.

Come January, Kim was planning to go back to her downtown office. Rob's paternity leave, which has allowed him to spend approximately fifty hours a week caring for Mackenzie, is up, and the nanny will be watching both children all day. The parents, who have thrived on this special time at home, face the transition with some trepidation. "I love to work, but I like it to be near my girls," says Kim. "For example, when Mattie Marie fell against the fence and cut her head, the nanny called down, and I was upstairs in a mini-second!"

Rob, acknowledging that his wife is the primary bread-winner and the person whose "income affords us a good lifestyle that would be impossible on my salary," feels he has made no major career sacrifice to be such a hands-on father. "Well," he grins, "maybe a little on-the-job teasing by coworkers for taking paternity leave." Some were envious and said so. "Others just looked at me, like 'You're a *guy*, what are you doing???' The women I work with—now they were totally supportive, like 'Right on!'"

What he does sacrifice for his involvement with his children is creative time, which includes digital photography, trip planning, and genealogical research. "When I have no time for creative things, I get depressed."

————

But some hands-on fathers do give up or postpone career dreams to be more family involved. Peter Groff, forty-four, a two-term state senator and executive director of the Center for African American Policy at the University of Denver, felt that he couldn't seriously consider the run for governor in 2006 that some leaders in the black community urged him to take on.

"It just wasn't the right time for the family," says Peter, whose wife, Regina, thirty-five, the first female pastor of an African Methodist Episcopal church in Denver, is trying to build her congregation's membership and to finish her doctorate. The Groffs have two children, Malachi Charles, six, who is in first grade, and Moriah Cherie, four, who is in preschool.

Peter estimates that he spends approximately thirty hours a week (less during the legislative session) in child-related activities. Regina adds that during the session when Peter served as president pro tem of the Senate, it was her job to get the kids off to school, as Peter needed to be at the Capitol at 7:30 or 8:00 in the morning, but that during the fall and summer months the responsibilities are more shared.

"I do more housework—I take out the trash and do all the laundry, though I'm behind!—and child rearing than my father did when I was growing up," says Peter. "And I make more career choices based on the demands of my wife's career."

Regina nods her head in appreciation, then comments that Peter's dad, former state senator Regis Groff, was a "true pioneer" in the African American community as only the second black state senator in Colorado history.

Both of these parents, who employ a cleaning service twice a month, are heavily into what would be termed "calling" careers, where the motivation comes from a "higher place" or a spiritual impetus. Nevertheless, each will give up important work-related meetings at a moment's notice for family time or child activities.

"I'm out of church meetings at 2:30 sharp every afternoon," says Regina, who in addition to cooking and tidying up after the kids, picks up the children from their schools and spends every afternoon with them, which often includes taking them to tae kwon do or piano lessons. "My staff and parishioners just expect that I leave at that time, and they know not to call me after 9 P.M. unless it is a true emergency."

"Will your constituents follow that rule?" I ask Peter.

"Well, many have my cell phone number."

"Do you answer it?"

"I think I've given most of them the wrong number," he says as he laughs, and Regina joins in. Turning serious, he admits that by putting his family first, he gives up "peripheral" meetings that could be important for networking, thus possibly missing some chances to progress further or faster or "to get even more involved—which would then *add* to the family pressures!"

Our interview took place on a busy weekday morning at Starbucks. Realizing I had been squeezed into their hectic and demanding schedule, I kept the visit to under an hour. Later in the day, I saw Peter at a political luncheon downtown. He flashed a wide grin as if to say, "Well, *sometimes* I go to meetings."

Earlier, at coffee, I had asked Peter if he regrets not running for governor. He pauses a moment. "Not really," he answers, "but the window of opportunity does close. ... "

And in politics that window often closes permanently. It is hard for me to imagine Peter's father, my husband, or any other male politician of my generation giving up their political goals to help their wives' careers or simply to be around more for their kids.

Dave Leuthold and Jenn Watts would be considered a dual-income couple; however, as Jenn clarifies with a laugh, "My income [as a second-year family medicine resident] only pays for the nanny!"

Dave, thirty-six, works forty-plus hours as a real estate broker, then comes home to spend twenty to thirty-five hours a week on child-related activities with their two daughters, Ruby, three and a half, and Vivian, one.

Devoted to his girls, Dave, whom I've known since his own early childhood, nevertheless sometimes resents the time he gives up at work: "When you are there more, you make more." He also finds the weekends Jenn is on hospital rotation tough. He deals with this situation by taking the girls to "visit Mommy at work in the hospital—which they love" and by "knowing that Jenn's time frame is not permanent."

In addition to much child nurturing, Dave cooks, cleans, and does yard work. A real outdoorsman, a great skier, and a lover of all physical activities, he occasionally thinks while raking the leaves or cleaning the fishpond, "So *this* is what my 'time off' is about?!"

But these gripes are said with a smile that seems genuine. In fact, as both Jenn and Dave, clothed in running pants and T-shirts, literally bounced into the teahouse to meet with me on a brisk Sunday afternoon in November, they exuded a sense of well-being, and as our conversation progressed, a basic satisfaction with life's current trade-offs.

Jenn, thirty-five, also an athlete who wishes she had more time to work out, spends sixty to eighty hours a week at her residency and then fifteen to forty more with the kids. Daughter of the late Dr. Thomas Watts, a Denver urologist who inspired her studies, she is dedicated to her career. However, when Jenn took two full years off between medical school and her residency after Ruby was born, she loved that too. "I wasn't bored at all."

Dave, who works in a male-dominated and conventional field, is sometimes teased by peers for having to "check with my wife" before going off with the guys on the spur of the moment. One Saturday, he and a close male friend, also married to a career wife, took their combined group of four little ones for a shopping venture at Costco. The trip turned into a mini-disaster, and as they kept the kids in tow crossing the parking lot, one of them invented the expression "I think I'm suffering the repercussions of decisions I don't make."

After Jenn's residency, they may decide to have a third child, and Jenn aspires to work in family medicine three days a week. "That feels like a breeze compared to now!" she exclaims.

"Yeah!" responds Dave with a look of relief and anticipation.

———

Dan Grossman and Robin Koenigsberg admit that they would be a couple charging full speed ahead—he in politics, she in business—if not for their children, Leah, age two, and Adin, five months.

As they sit in the sun-filled living room of their new home, with Leah asleep upstairs and Adin murmuring contentedly in his father's arms, they speak poignantly about their priorities and their lives. Dan, thirty-nine, regional director and senior attorney at Environmental Defense in Boulder and a former state senator, had planned to run for attorney general in 2006. But the "price was too high," and he changed his mind.

"We simply realized that the AG job would take 40 percent more time, I'd earn 40 percent less money, and I would be multitasking *all* the time."

Although his job in Boulder is a forty-five-minute commute, Dan revels in the fact that, aside from the days he leaves early to pick up the children at day care, "When I'm home, I'm home, and I don't have to work after hours."

Robin, age thirty-six, who holds an MA in international trade and economic development and a PhD in economics, is an assistant professor of economics at Regis University. She admits, however, that if it were not for their young children, she might still be in the corporate world. In fact, her former employer, Sun Microsystems, allowed her to shift to a part-time job-share situation, but because of the short-deadline nature of the corporate job, she moved into academia, despite the flextime advantages and much higher salary Sun Microsystems offered.

"In the corporate world, as in politics, you just have to be 'on' all the time—it's so stimulating it just takes over your life!"

Robin, who works thirty-five to forty hours a week, ten of them in planning courses and grading papers after the babies are in bed, says she knows only a few women with children who are employed at the kind of corporate job she used to have. All the rest are single and/or childless.

"When would you see them?!" she implores, hands rising to match the inflection in her voice, then adds that in the corporate world she often worked nights, weekends, and vacations.

Right now Dan and Robin, who is still breast-feeding, figure they each spend between forty and forty-five hours a week with their children or in child-related activities, and that is their priority. Like Peter and Regina Groff, whom they know well through politics, Dan and Robin are imbued with the ethic of contributing to society. And although to most observers their current professional positions would appear mighty contributory, they see their major contribution at this time as "being with and raising good kids."

As if on cue after this statement from Dan, Leah cries out from upstairs, signaling that she is awake. Quickly Dan hands Adin to Robin and bounds upstairs to bring sleepy-eyed Leah down. Once again I am amazed at how this couple—just like Renate and Eric, and Stephanie and Jon—can lavish affection on their little ones, passing them naturally from one to the other, without missing a beat in the conversation.

But sometimes, the omnipresent cell phone, BlackBerry, or Palm Pilot can interfere with this ease, whether parents are trying to converse with other adults or simply attempting to be with their children.

Jim and Lisa Merlino, who live in Broomfield, Colorado, took time from their fully packed schedules to meet me at a coffeehouse in southeast Denver. Jim is there first and quickly turns off his cell as I approach. Then Lisa arrives in a rush, apologizing for being late, although she isn't. This is the same couple described earlier who had blown me away when Dad checked his BlackBerry to see when the baby had last been fed.

We immediately get into it. Jim says they had worked out their roles and their kids' schedules "pretty smoothly," and Lisa retorts, "except for this weekend!"

Jim looks blank.

"You were totally unavailable and always on the cell phone!" She exclaims.

"Hmmm … yes, guess I was," Jim agrees.

Then Lisa, who first met Jim while working on the 1996 Clinton-Gore presidential campaign, comes quickly to his defense and notes that he was "not usually that way."

It was the weekend after the 2006 election, and Jim, a political consultant for a candidate who had lost, had a series of mandatory debriefing conference calls typical for anyone in his profession. Lisa admits that she, too, had "totally lost it" once toward the end of one of the campaigns Jim was working on: for the first time ever, after a long work day, she had to call her mother to come over and take care of the girls, as she wasn't sure she could handle the evening routine without him.

Jim, forty-seven, who is a real estate broker as well a political consultant, works from home 50 to 60 percent of his time. On top of that, he figures he spends an additional forty-two hours a week on child-related activities for Maggie, three years, and Allison, seven months. A favorite activity is reading to the girls before bedtime, though Maggie will no longer tolerate his favorite book, *Hippos Go Berserk!*, because he has overread it.

"I missed half of Maggie's first year of life, working in Pueblo for Congressman John Salazar's congressional campaign in 2004," says Jim. "I was *not* going to do that with Allison," he adds vehemently. "My current schedule allows me to stay closer to home." Jim was raised around four strong women and "was a feminist before I was!" says Lisa, whose eyes sparkle whether talking about her husband, her daughters, or her job.

As the deputy director of Invest in Kids, a Denver-based child advocacy organization, Lisa, thirty-five, works at her job thirty-two hours a week, then figures she spends close to fifty hours with her two daughters or on activities related to their care.

"Gender roles aren't our deal," says Jim, who does most of the grocery shopping and cooking, not only because his schedule is more flexible, but also because he likes it. He adds that "one parent having flexibility can make all the difference in the world."

Yet Jim and Lisa, like all the dual-income families interviewed, do rely at least half-time on alternate care. For them, an aunt comes in on Monday, a nanny on Tuesday, Wednesday, and Thursday, and then Lisa takes all of Friday off.

Lisa says that neither one of them tries to work and watch the children at the same time. "They won't tolerate it from me," she says. "Last week I walked in the house on my cell phone after work and Maggie immediately realized I was distracted and got frustrated and upset within seconds."

Jim, because he is twelve years older than Lisa, feels he is in a "different place in his career."

"He sets better boundaries," adds Lisa. "He can go into his study, shut the door, and Maggie just accepts it, happy to be with me or the nanny. I, on the other hand, respond quickly to every little need and hover—you know, like this … " She rises and bends over the table with her eyes peering down and her arms flapping like a momma bird over her nest.

We all laugh, and Lisa and I wonder if some responses have just got to be gender specific and biologically ingrained. Jim is not convinced.

"Oh, come on!" says Lisa. "Hovering is a carryover from breast-feeding; when either of the girls would cry, the milk would let down—an immediate response—and I would need to feed them to relieve the pressure."

She says that despite Jim's amazing flexibility, he really does think everything can be controlled. "Like when I was in hard labor with Maggie, he said to me, 'If the contractions are that hard, why don't you just skip the next one?' Can you believe it?"

This kind of joshing humor, sprinkled throughout our interview, communicates the closeness in their relationship, despite the spats. In fact, when I left the coffee shop they didn't rush off, but lingered at the table, eager and engaged in catching up on their day so far.

It is clear that Jim may be giving up some political opportunities to maintain strong relationships with his family, yet he appears to have few regrets. Despite total dedication to their daughters, neither Jim nor Lisa would choose to make homemaking and child care their full-time careers. Thanks to their coparenting approach and the quality caregivers they rely on, they feel they can balance their careers and family life.

"There are days when I envy people who can parent full-time," says Jim. "It's hard work, but it's very fulfilling."

———

Next, I've got three fathers, who, along with the two stay-at-home mothers described earlier, have decided to parent full-time.

Are they fulfilled? Overworked? Perhaps both?

Let's see ...

Chapter Three
Daddy Full-Time

Will Fay, forty-nine, Dessa Bokides, forty-eight, and their four boys live in a spacious, gracious home—a house that would overwhelm by its size if it were not for its comfortable, rambling quality and natural outdoor space.

I had first read of Dessa Bokides, the former chief financial officer of the international real estate investment trust ProLogis, in the business section of *The Denver Post*, September 3, 2006. Here was a woman who traveled extensively, cofounded The Hidden Brain Drain (a task force sponsored by the Center for Work-Life Policy), had a family of four boys and a husband who has stayed home to care for them since the second one was born in 1992. "I've got to meet her!" I thought.

Interviewing Dessa in the spacious conference room at ProLogis, I ask what had led to the decision for Will to become a full-time dad.

There were "nanny problems," she answers, and since he wasn't as satisfied with his job at the time as she was with hers, he figured he'd quit and stay home "for a while."

Dessa, raised on a ranch in Idaho, and Will, a suburbanite from Bedford, New York, met on a ski trip when both were attending Columbia Business School. Surprised that Will could move so quickly from the trained-by-Columbia business world to the baby world, I ask Dessa to elaborate on that decision.

She laughs and says he just told people that he had

"gone from bossing eighteen people around to letting an eighteen-month-old boss him around." Stopping herself and laughing again, she says, "Maybe you better ask him."

So I called him, and he invited me out to their home for further conversation. As Will motions for me to sit down in the cozy family room where his oldest son does his homework, he tells of his family's journey: from Manhattan, where Dessa worked at Goldman Sachs; to Stamford, Connecticut, when their first child was born; then later, to Greenwich, Connecticut; and finally, in 2005, to Colorado.

Then he relates his personal journey as a full-time stay-at-home dad. When Dessa first suggested he might stay home, he was taken back. "No way!" he said. But then he started to think about it. "I didn't like the direction my small business partnership was headed, and, bottom line, it seemed like just the right thing to do for the family."

But "stay-at-home" is hardly the way to describe Will Fay's approach to parenting. By the time the third boy came along, in 1994, Will had become adept at organizing playdates, taking the boys on excursions to parks and museums, and volunteering in the community. He also hired a part-time babysitter so that he could occasionally get out with just one child or on his own.

"You know, when you have only one child you can still have your own life. When you have two you can *pretend* that you still have your own life. But when you have three, your life is *gone*!"

> "You know, when you have only one child you can still have your own life. When you have two you can *pretend* that you still have your own life. But when you have three, your life is *gone!*"
> —Will Fay

When the boys started preschool, Will joined the board of trustees and volunteered to oversee some school building and construction projects. When the first two entered the public elementary school, the mothers of the other kids ignored him, so he ran for president of the PTA and won. Grinning, he adds that his victory was actually by acclamation. "No one else really wanted the job." But he found, as his wife had already suggested to him, that once he was president, no one could afford to ignore him. As the boys grew, he not only continued to keep things going on the home and school fronts, but he also became president of the Greenwich Travel Soccer League, in which his children were involved.

The family moved to Denver for Dessa's high-level job offer at ProLogis, which, of course, meant uprooting their four children, now ages ten to fifteen, and enrolling them in brand-new schools. Although they had gone without household help for many years, the family has again hired a nanny to help with the various after-school activities of four active boys all going in different directions. Will said that it might be different with girls, but it was very hard to "program" his boys. That's why he is glad to be around every afternoon for conversations and homework help and to see to their emotional needs as they arise. "It just doesn't cut it to come in late in the afternoon and say, 'How was your day?'"

Dessa, who, with the help of a nanny, worked from home one day a week with their first baby, says she had some trouble letting go when Will took over. Describing herself as very organized, she remembers coming home one night and being somewhat bothered to find the boys in their beds, every single one of them in unmatched pajama tops and bottoms.

She noted the mismatch to Will, who replied, "They are happy and asleep. What difference does it make?" She smiles with a shrug that seems to say she has learned not to sweat the small stuff.

Will laughs fondly when I mention the pajama story, but adds that she has a little more trouble letting go of a kitchen organized her way. "Women seem much more interested than men in having the kitchen arranged just the way they want it," he says.

So here's this caretaking dad, who has lived most of his parenting life in the upscale communities of Greenwich, Connecticut, and Cherry Hills Village, Colorado—areas where moms are usually full-time homemakers and dads go out into the business world each day. Yet Will has found that even in such an atmosphere, their communities have seemed to accept their unconventional choice.

There was, however, one incident years ago when the husband of a neighbor would not let his wife arrange playdates with Will because he was suspicious of "what might go on."

"Can you imagine?!" he says, laughing and shaking his head in disbelief. "Here we are with three preschoolers each, *six* total, running around, and we're going to be sneaking to an upstairs bedroom or something!"

This incident was mystifying and painful at the time, though later Will and Dessa became good friends with the couple who had denied him playdates. Generally, Will has felt little prejudice or isolation over the years and is presently becoming involved in the school community of his younger children.

Also, Will's parents, both public school teachers, totally approve of his at-home role. "They appreciate kids, whether their own or their students," says Will, "and they understand how much attention children need." Will and his dad spent lots of time together when he was growing up, mainly hiking the trails and climbing the mountains of Vermont and New Hampshire, though he said that his dad was not a nurturing type of father when he and his siblings were little. "This probably made me more aware of the need to be one."

Dessa and Will have little time together as a couple. In

the positions she has held, she has found her job and travel schedule so demanding that when she is home, she wants to be with the boys as much as possible. As a family, they ski together almost every other weekend, and during summers they spend at least two weeks at the ranch she grew up on in Idaho.

What are Will's plans for the future? Most likely, to get involved in a major board, volunteer his efforts for a children's advocacy or environmental organization, or a combination of these.

As I close this section, I receive an e-mail from Dessa saying she has resigned her position at ProLogis, but that family issues were not the reason. Her plans remain undecided at this time.

———

As I sit at the hardwood dining room table of Sandra Donnell and Kent Gardener's restored central-Denver house, I flash back to Dick's and my first home.

Such similarities in lifestyle!

Such differences in professions and roles!

I cannot imagine myself, younger, as a full-time physician like Sandra, and my husband a stay-at-home dad like Kent. In fact, in those days, I think we knew only one female doctor—the wife of Dick's law partner.

In 1974, when a good female friend of mine tried to enter a renowned medical school, the dean of the school, a harsh, unmarried, childless woman, said, "Yes, you are probably qualified, but you must know that a medical career will certainly break up your marriage and ruin your four-year-old son's life for good."

My friend backed off and let go of her career dreams.

Did we know any full-time-dad homemakers? None that I can remember. And if we had, we probably would have assumed he was a wussy or simply biding time 'til he found his next "real" job.

Thirty years later, I see that Sandra and Kent are content, at least for now, with their roles and choices, and although different from most of their friends, they don't feel highly unusual.

Kent, a former recording engineer in Hollywood who worked with such notables as Barbra Streisand, tired of his gig and enrolled in the School of Architecture at Washington University in Saint Louis. There he met Sandra, a third-year resident at the Saint Louis University Hospital. Upon completion of her residency, the couple moved to Denver in 2000, where Sandra immediately went to work for Denver Health as an urgent care physician and is still there today. They married in 2001. Kent went to work for Humphries Poli Architects, but was laid off in the post-9/11 building and construction recession. The layoff came on their second anniversary and right after Sandra suffered a miscarriage—indeed a traumatic time.

Kent then started his own architecture business from his home office, and Sandra became pregnant with Chris, born in June of 2004, now two and a half years old. Kent's home-business arrangement worked throughout Chris's infancy, he says, but as his son grew, "I found it almost impossible to get my work done." So Sandra, then pregnant with Amy, now ten months old, spent almost every hour of her days off keeping toddler Chris occupied and away from home so that Kent could work—"Very tiring!" she adds.

Then, when the project deadline loomed for a large historical assessment of a neighborhood church, the pressure on both of them reached crisis proportions. Sandra, thirty-eight, a soft-spoken brunette whose serene manner is often broken by a contagious laugh, says, "Thank heavens my mom could come from Missouri for two weeks to help out!"

Kent, who at forty-three is tall, athletic, and still has the relaxed look and demeanor of a college student, is visibly comfortable about his decision to give up the architectural business completely and care for his two children full-time. He does employ a babysitter two afternoons a week, not to pursue his career, but for creative endeavors such as photography, model train building, and a newly acquired aquarium. Once a tuba player for the San Diego Youth Symphony, Kent now plays the guitar and banjo. Will he parlay any of these into future professional work? Maybe … but not now.

When the sitter comes and Kent wants to hole up in his study, he has to leave the house, say good-bye to the children, and then sneak back into his privacy. His kids will *not* tolerate a closed door with a parent behind it!

Everything in their lives must be worked around Sandra's schedule, which is updated a month in advance on a dry-erase board posted prominently on the freezer door. She works an average of forty-five to forty-eight hours a week, and her shift is different every day.

Our interview took place on a cold winter night at nine o'clock. The children were asleep upstairs, and the day had been a long one. Although they were most gracious, I sensed that it might have been a real effort to add one more thing—my interview—to their load. Kent and Sandra divide up the day-to-day housework in their recently remodeled home, where the walls are alive with charming professional photographs of the four of them as a family.

Sandra does the laundry. Kent does the dishes and takes out the trash. Although Kent likes to cook, Sandra prefers taking the kids out for sushi or to one of the numerous inexpensive family-friendly restaurants in the area. The hard and grimy housework became an issue between them, so they hired a cleaning person for one day every other week.

Kent does miss the income he has given up. And some of their few disagreements center on how much he can now spend on his "toys," especially the equipment for his many hobbies. Yet to Kent, whatever the sacrifices, they are worth it.

"What makes my day is seeing them learn something new, or reach a new milestone," Kent writes about his children in a follow up e-mail. "Today, Chris learned how to open the stair gates we installed for protection. Although it means we have to be more careful to be sure they are closed for Amy, I am proud that he figured out how they work."

Not that there aren't downsides to daddy care. For instance, "As soon as the kids get big enough to roll over and put up a fight, some diaper changes feel like a bout of Greco-Roman wrestling with poop involved. That is when I start to feel angry and frustrated." Another thing that gets him down is "when both kids are crying at the same time, usually because they want to do something they can't. It makes me feel like I'm out of control."

> "What makes my day is seeing them learn something new, or reach a new milestone."
> —Kent Gardener

Both Sandra's and Kent's parents approve of their role choices and are simply glad that one person can stay home with the kids. Neither Sandra nor Kent, both from middle-class, professional families, has ever felt undue pressure from their folks about anything. Only Kent's maternal grandmother, still "smart and aware" well into her eighties, worries that he may not pursue architecture. "You know," he says with a smile that seems solicitous of Grandma, "I was her first male grandchild. ... "

Sandra and Kent maintain a social life with couples from their church and Sandra's work, with other parents of small children, and with a close male friend who took their whole family into his home when theirs was being remodeled. Do they take the children with them on social occasions? "No!" replies Sandra, who had arranged our interview at a time she knew the children would be in bed. "We all get babysitters and leave them home!" Kent grins with approval, and Sandra adds later, "I think we go out with friends so we can keep some [friends] and for both of our mental states."

Despite her workload, Sandra spends almost every other waking moment with the children, so the outings with adults become a way for them to touch base with the outside world and get a reality check. Kent does feel isolated at times (he wrote on his questionnaire that he has difficulty developing and maintaining outside friend-ships) much like some stay-at-home moms do, but with a different, even more isolating twist. Because he is male, the mothers at Chris's preschool ignored him at first, similar to Will Fay's experience.

"It was like I just wasn't there!" he says. "I felt more rapport with the nannies who brought kids in," he reports, adding that he could understand that the moms had their own preexisting in-group. "But they're more used to me now," he continues.

When a male friend responded to his new stay-at-home status with, "Well! I just can't relate to that," Kent felt only "temporarily taken aback," but Sandra was "thoroughly insulted. ... He shouldn't have been so judgmental!"

Kent doesn't much miss his associates or the culture at the architectural firm. "The tension was really high in those days of incessant and impending layoffs," he says. If he does go back to paid work, he may look for some kind of a third career. In the meantime, he appears in no hurry.

———

Paul LeFever seems in no hurry either, though he has been an almost full-time stay-at-home dad since he and his wife,

Karen, moved to Colorado in 1999. Their children, Bryan, seventeen, and Elizabeth, fourteen, see this role of their dad's as "no problem," although occasionally, says Karen, who travels in her work, they regard Dad as "over the top protective" about what they are doing and where they are going. She will occasionally get a text message from one of them saying, "MOM—tell Dad to back off!!"

Karen, forty-five, a former schoolteacher and principal of Wyatt Edison Charter School in northeast Denver, is currently senior vice president of sales and marketing for Educational Services of America. Paul, forty-seven, is a former church youth director. They moved to Colorado because they wanted a change.

"We both grew up in Southern California, and we thought a change would be great for all of us—even the weather," says Paul. "It was the best thing we ever did!"

We all laugh as we look out the huge, wood-framed window of their house at the barely melting snowfield after yet another mid-February storm. It is a Saturday morning, and both teenagers are asleep upstairs. In this temporarily child-free interlude, both Karen and Paul seem energized and eager to share their stories.

Karen, a tall, vivacious blond, and Paul, a classically handsome man with the same muscular build that made him a good water polo player in high school, met at a YMCA summer camp where he was working as a camp manager and she was counseling for a week while obtaining her BS at the University of Southern California.

"I thought, 'Wow! Who is that good-looking guy driving the tractor?'" says Karen. What could have been a summer romance turned serious, and they married a year later. They have been married twenty-one years.

Paul, who did not have a college degree, completed his BA in business administration and e-commerce through the University of Phoenix in 2002. Looking fondly at a photo of his two children—arms around him, smiles broad, as he, in graduation gown, holds up his diploma for the world to see—Paul says, "I desperately want my kids to go to college, so I needed to be an example for them."

In some ways, the LeFever family's life has always had its nontraditional elements, especially compared to Karen's upper-middle-class childhood in Newport Beach, where most moms were homemakers. When the kids were little, they made do with Karen's maternity leave, Paul's irregular hours, a nanny two days a week, and day care. But since the day care was at the church where Paul worked, the kids thought of it not as day care, but simply "going to work with Daddy."

"In a way, I'm wired for this," says Paul, who is a night owl and only needs about six hours of sleep. "Last night, for example, I fixed dinner, took Elizabeth and her friends to a movie, and then waited up nervously for Bryan, who now drives, to come home."

"And I," says Karen, who had just returned from a business trip, "was dead asleep by 10 P.M.!"

Paul's father was extremely strict and demanding; he remembers being spanked by his dad when he couldn't ride his tricycle at age three. He is adamant about never using physical discipline with his kids. "My mom was smart enough to flee with us when I was six and my baby sister was only two months."

Paul, who was then raised by his mother and his aunts, says pensively that maybe it is easier for him to be in the nurturing role since he was raised by women. Paul's mom remarried when he was thirteen. When he graduated from high school at eighteen, Paul's folks told him he was on his own; there was no encouragement to go to college. He turned to what he'd been doing for many summers and got full-time work at the YMCA.

Today he brings some of those Y skills to his summer

job as manager of the outdoor recreation center at Grant Ranch. This, again, allows him more involvement with and supervision of his teenagers, who participate there. It also gives him more social contact with the community.

The couple has made friends in the area, but it's been slow. Compared to their conservative community in California, their rambling, almost rural Colorado suburb tends toward the middle, politically and religiously. However, a small group of religious conservatives in their neighborhood do not approve of Karen and Paul's lifestyle.

> "When people ask what I do," says Paul LeFever, "it is so much easier to say, 'I'm self-employed' or 'I work out of my home,' but I try not to." Sometimes he feels defensive and wants to say, "If you only *knew* what I do!" But he doesn't.

"When people ask what I do," says Paul, "it is so much easier to say, 'I'm self-employed' or 'I work out of my home,' but I try not to." Sometimes he feels defensive and wants to say, "If you only *knew* what I do!" But he doesn't.

Karen interrupts. "Can you believe that in this day and age, some people see a man who takes care of his kids as a bad example for *their* kids—not just that is 'odd,' but that it's 'morally wrong'!"

"These are male-dominant/female-subservient families," says Paul, who admits he enjoys being the only dad who's a room mom. "Such reactions have made us teach our own children that each gender has an equal choice and each family can make its own decisions."

Do they feel they are actually shunned by some neighbors? Paul hesitates and thinks a minute. But Karen says, "Yes! I'll give you an example."

It seems that the husband of a woman in the neighborhood whom Karen had gotten close to was giving his wife a surprise birthday party. When Karen met the woman on the street a few days later, the woman greeted her with, "Hi, Karen! I was surprised you and Paul weren't at my birthday party!"

When Karen said gently that they hadn't known about it—that they hadn't been invited, the woman blanched and looked so embarrassed that Karen felt sorry for her and said no more. A couple of weeks later, a mutual friend told them the exclusion was because of their reversed mom and dad roles.

Looking to the future, Paul knows he will not go back to youth counseling in a church, as "the church takes too many of your weekends." But with his business degree, his recreation center experience, his past job in counseling, and his dedication to the welfare of kids, his own and others, he knows he'll find something engaging and challenging in the youth field.

———

Although these three dads have weathered, with a shrug or a laugh, the few incidents of scorn directed at them for taking on the role of prime parent (their wives seem more offended at the scorn than they do), many other men do not fare as well.

Recently, Dick and I ran into a psychologist friend who sees a good number of stay-at-home dads in couples therapy. "Ultimately they are depressed," she says, and they have "issues of low self-esteem and feelings that they aren't measuring up."

"Wives become resentful too," she adds. "'Why do *I* have to support the entire family?' or 'I want more family time too!' are typical attitudes."

We then laugh as we suddenly realize that "our" couples had to be somewhat self-selecting. They come to her, a therapist, with problems and want to share their pain in private. They come to me, a journalist, with success stories and want to share their pleasures with the world.

The psychologist's husband, who is listening to our

conversation, laughs and looks at my husband, who is also tuned in. "Dick," he says, "we escaped! Thank God we grew away from those new expectations just in time."

Yes, but the old expectations still linger.

Former attorney and corporate career coach Leslie Hilton says sometimes role-switching is a matter of necessity; if so, it is more likely to work. She tells of a couple she counseled, a corporate executive wife on the fast track and her health-care professional husband who was bored with his job. A "natural nurturer," he decided to work part-time and take on the major home-care responsibility for their middle-school-age son and daughter. Immediately he had self-image problems "being out in the stores shopping with the housewives."

And his wife had issues with "that unconscious woman thing—the man goes out and slays the dragon, and the woman, well, she does what she chooses," even though her own parents admonished, "What's the problem? You love each other. He's a great husband—make it work!"

Things were still rocky, but then the husband found he had a serious health condition that mandated a low-key schedule. All of a sudden, pulling back from a career was okay because it was medically indicated, perhaps for his survival. The couple took another look and said, "Why are we doing what we are doing?"

He resigned even the part-time work and learned to do everything around the house and for the kids. Turning to a long unused creative bent, he invested energy in landscape planning, graphic design, and even started shopping for his wife's business attire, as he felt her sartorial instincts had never matched her position or her business acumen. Now, with his daughter in college and his son a junior in high school, he's feeling the empty-nest syndrome more than his wife is.

Leslie emphasized that in order for the couple to make

their choice a comfortable one, it was the dad's medical condition that allowed all the "superficial image stuff to peel away." When role change can be lifesaving, you just do it!

Yet, as Karen and Paul LeFever discovered, the "superficial image stuff" still surrounds us. And no wonder! Compared to the 24 percent of married moms who stay home full-time, only .7 percent of married dads do the same. Although, according to the U.S. Census Bureau, this figure does represent a tripling of stay-at-home dads from 49,000 in 1996 to 159,000 in 2006, the present number can hardly be considered a critical mass. And perhaps only a critical mass of stay-at-home dads at the middle-income professional level will make "male homemaking" acceptable, respectable, and "normal." ·

Researchers do estimate that if one took into account the fathers who work part-time or those who work from home, the number of stay-at-home dads who manage both kids and household would be closer to 2 million, which inches us a little closer to critical mass.

And already we've come a long way from Michael Keaton's 1983 depiction of the bumbling stay-at-home father in the movie *Mr. Mom*. As journalist Jocelyne ZablitSun wrote in the blog at www.daddyfu.jelyon.com, "While it may have popularized the term, the film treated the species as an oddity, a stay-at-home dad who is there because he lost his job, struggling to cope with diaper-changing, meal-cooking and home multi-tasking handled 'easily' by women."

Today, according to ZablitSun, as the number of stay-at-home dads and single dads with sole custody of the children grows, so does the number of support groups, playgroups, and blogs. In Colorado, father of four Jim Turner has started such a blog at www.genuineblog.com, and its highly amusing content (the trials and tribulations of his family, punctuated by memorable movie quotes) continues to be popular among readers.

There is, of course, the issue of money. In all five single-income couples interviewed (three with Dad at home and two with Mom at home), the person in the workplace was not only making more money at the time the decision was made, but was also in a career guaranteed to continue to be more lucrative than that of her or his spouse.

But money is only part of it. Thirty percent of all wives in the paid workforce now earn more money than their husbands. And 42 percent of college-educated wives earn a higher income than their spouses. According to one report, a majority of men reported that they "wouldn't mind"—and some even "would like it"—if their wives made more money than they did!

Compared to the "Watch What You Wish For" stories of the early nineties, when it was likely that a woman's income shooting ahead of her husband's would lead to divorce, recent divorce data, according to commentators at www.womensenews.org, indicates that "these marriages are as stable as those in which husbands earn more." Still, seldom does a husband use his wife's higher income as a reason to stay out of the paid workforce himself.

And many men (59 percent, in fact, according to the staffing firm Adecco U.S.A.) "won't even take paid paternity leave, fearing harm to their careers or pocketbooks," writes *Denver Post* business columnist Al Lewis.

Researcher Aaron Rochlen, associate professor of psychology at the University of Texas who specializes in research on men and masculinity, says that of the 213 stay-at-home dads who took part in his study, those who seemed to be struggling more with their role were men who adhere to traditional norms of masculinity. On the flip side, men who adhered more to flexible male gender roles than to traditional ones seemed to adjust well to their role as stay-at-home fathers.

A single female friend of mine who has no children but dotes on her nieces and nephews mused for a moment when I mentioned the characteristics of the stay-at-home dads in my study. She then commented, "Both of my brothers stay home with their kids, and it's made them not only better fathers, but better people."

Nurturing Fathers: A "Natural" Phenomenon?

Then there is the eternal question: Is nurturing natural to men? If not, can it be learned?

Will Fay, who has learned one heck of a lot about nurturing in the last sixteen years, still thinks some things are hardwired by sex. He and I have both read the studies revealing that women's hearing is more fine-tuned, that women can hear more sounds simultaneously than men, and that their natural auditory superiority often translates to heightened responsiveness and sharpened nurturing skills.

I once wrote a column called "Moms Hear Better!" based on the time when, as houseguests of friends, I woke at six in the morning to the sound of clip, clip, clip. Looking over the railing of the bedroom loft into the living room, I gasped as I saw our two-and-a-half-year-old son, Scott, decimating our hosts' houseplant with a pair of twelve-inch shears. I gasped again when I saw his father sitting ten feet away, totally absorbed in the Sunday *New York Times*.

Is this male deafness or male focus? Could Dick have trained himself to pick up such subtle danger signals?

Maybe dads wouldn't even need to train themselves to be more attentive nurturers if they would just spend more snuggle time with their new infants, for it has been recently found that early baby-bonding with dads (just like with moms) has its own hormonal component. Toward the end of a partner's pregnancy, "human males are known to have high levels of prolactin (a hormone usually associated with lactating mothers)," writes anthropologist Sarah Blaffer

Hrdy in a June 8, 2007, *Time* article.

And Canadian biologist Katherine Wynne-Edwards and psychologist Anne Storey, quoted in the same article, found that new or expectant dads "holding either their baby or a doll wrapped in a blanket that recently held—and still smells of—a newborn experienced a rise in prolactin and cortisol (a well-known stress hormone associated with mothering) and a drop in testosterone."

But Dad does have to spend time with the baby, or a doll that smells like baby, for the nurturing hormones to kick in. Sorry, guys, but I doubt that carrying that blanket-wrapped doll to work will go over with your associates. Nor is it likely to be considered equal baby-care time by your wife—not when she's home with the real one!

One does have to wonder if, once those hormones have kicked in (or out, as with testosterone), would the dads, then, just like moms, retain that acute child awareness after the hormonal influence had faded away?

In the meantime, Will Fay says that women are more likely to see the big picture regarding children and to not be impelled to make all decisions immediately; that, in the workplace as well, they (and he cites his wife Dessa as an example) can tell the difference between what *truly* needs to be decided quickly and what needs to be decided quickly only to please the comfort level of the males around the table. He feels this "natural" ability of hers has made her a more effective, forward-thinking executive. And the fact that he has been able to learn this skill has made him a better parent.

Our son, Scott—of earlier plant-clipping fame—now thirty-nine and a first-time father of baby Kennon, feels he is just not the same kind of parent his wife, Cindy, is, no matter how much time he puts in.

"She's 'with him' all the time," he says. "I feed him, talk to him, change him, play with him, and be sure he is safe, then I go on to other things. I just couldn't give him the complete attention she does."

"Couldn't or wouldn't?" I ask. And then I tell him about the full-time fathers I've been interviewing. He shakes his head in both respect and wonder. "I just don't have that constant baby concentration."

A dad ten years my senior, a pioneer who raised his children as a single parent in the early 1960s, insists that the drastic changes in the last thirty years with husbands taking on multifaceted nurturing and domestic duties proves that these roles can't all be biologically hardwired. If they were, the changes couldn't have happened so fast. And another father I know, a teacher ten years my junior who took the primary care of both of his sons (now grown) since infancy because of his wife's demanding legal career, is convinced there is no role, duty, or function after the first six months of life that can't be done equally well by either gender.

Some men will do the complete nurturing. Some will not. Some will say they can. Some will say they can't. But it is my bet that all dedicated fathers could nurture well if they had to. After all, look at the early pioneer women, who, assuming they would still be traditional ladies, brought their fine china to the West in covered wagons. Yet when their husbands died, they forgot about the cherished dinnerware and took over the management of the family sheep and cattle ranches. They had to, so they did. And some of them did it damn well.

Alan LaBranche, a single dad raising two young daughters, spoke about his budding intuition to *The New York Times* for a story on Father's Day 2001. Predating by three years Rob Carmody's ability to see the signs, LaBranche says, "I know when they're sick; I know when they're upset and I ask what's wrong. I think that's developing in fathers now, whereas ten years ago it was nonexistent."

So, while this is all evolving, let's treat stay-at-home dads with the same respect we treat stay-at-home moms.

But wait a minute! Isn't this aiming too low? Do we, in fact, treat any of the unpaid caretaking roles in our country with respect? We might, especially on the individual level, but our society as a whole does not.

The Web site www.salary.com estimates that if we did pay a wage to a stay-at-home parent of one preschooler and one school-age child, the jobs he or she does would be worth between $128,775 and $138,095 a year. But alas, we do *not* pay them!

However, maybe our negative attitude toward home-makers or caretakers of either sex doesn't tell the whole story. For where we might demean dads more for staying home, it seems we demean moms for whatever role they choose.

On to the Mommy Wars!

Chapter Four
What Source, the Mommy Wars?

Jenn Watts, her eight-month-old daughter clinging to her neck, whining and climbing as if flames were lapping at her feet, tried to detach herself long enough to say good-bye to her older daughter's preschool teacher.

Another preschool mother said pointedly, "She wouldn't cling like that if you didn't work."

"Stomach stab! That's what it felt like," says Jenn. "The minute I got in the car, I picked up my cell phone and dialed my pediatrician for advice and reassurance."

"Jennifer," the pediatrician said, "eight-month-olds *cling.*"

Jenn laughs and says that as a mother of two and a physician-in-training herself, she should have been more secure, but she wasn't.

That's one thing that hasn't changed much over the decades—mommy insecurity and mommy guilt.

Perhaps it's in our cultural DNA. I think of Sarah Orne Jewett's 1884 novel *A Country Doctor*, which poignantly depicts the heroine having to choose *between* pursuing her medical career or marrying and having children. In those days there would have been no Jenn Watts taking a break from her hospital residency to pick up her daughter at preschool. She would have been Mrs. David Leuthold, wife and mother, *or* Jennifer Watts, MD in training.

Now we do not have to choose between these lives— one unfulfilled professionally and the other forever lonely and bereft of family—but we can be catapulted into guilt about *any* choice or combination of choices that we do make. And our insecurity, coiled like a sleeping serpent in our unconscious, is eager to spring when we are stomach stabbed by another mother, perhaps defending her own insecure turf.

Jenn's husband, Dave, weighed in about the other mother: "That was her problem, not yours! Why did you even have to take it on?"

The three of us then digressed into a full-blown discussion of how women take on fault as their own, whereas men project fault onto others or onto circumstances. Stereotypical, of course, and yet I have never met a dad in this project or in any generation who ever exhibited guilt over a child-related role he did or did not take on.

Men's feelings about time spent (or not spent) with their kids may range from joy, sorrow, frustration, isolation, inspiration, exhaustion, exhilaration, to occasional regret or resentment—but rarely guilt. Whatever power men may feel they have lost due to the feminist revolution, they still exhibit a sense of entitlement: I can make this decision, right or wrong. If it's wrong I can change it, but no second-guessing. No wasting time in guilt.

> Whatever power men may feel they have lost due to the feminist revolution, they still exhibit a sense of entitlement: I can make this decision, right or wrong. If it's wrong I can change it, but no second-guessing. No wasting time in guilt.

Maybe for women, guilt and insecurity in our motherhood roles comes from female-family DNA. Women keep their own moms, living or dead, and their moms' parenting of them tight inside themselves like a subtle (or not-so-subtle) genetic blueprint. This almost symbiotic "memory" is not necessarily a negative phenomenon! In fact, that mother-daughter closeness is the umbilical cord that binds, that passes on nurturing skills. But sometimes the cord can bind too tightly, whether the mom of the mom means it to or not.

"Moms want to please their mothers," says Laurie Weiss, PhD, a world-renowned psychotherapist and job coach. "I have to watch how I make suggestions to my daughter [a career woman with four boys ranging in age from one to eight years]. They can be interpreted as criticism, even though that's not at all how I mean them."

She told how she had to counter her own mom's disapproval of her beginning her career when her two children were still young. Laurie and her husband and counseling partner, Jonathan Weiss, coparented from the beginning, and her mom, who started a very successful career later in life, just didn't get it. "So I sat down and wrote her a long letter saying that I really admired what she had done and that I was doing exactly what she had programmed me to do, only ten years earlier."

Some moms don't resolve their inner or outer conflicts with their own moms until it's almost too late. A friend my age who died five years ago realized her professional dream late in life. She went back to school—the University of Denver's Graduate School of Social Work—when the last of her three children went off to college, and she became a talented and respected therapist. Once I asked why she hadn't gone back to school earlier, for instance when her kids were in middle school.

"It had nothing to do with my children," she said. "It was my mother. I couldn't face the pressure of her opinion that a married woman should stay home and be a perfect wife, no matter what ... so I didn't go back to school until she died."

Then *she* died fifteen years later. A brilliant career, but tragically too short.

Mandates, real or imagined, from our mothers have eased as the generations have passed, but not entirely. I find it intriguing that the original modern feminist, Betty Friedan, who in 1963 published the culture-changing book *The Feminine Mystique*—which urged housewives to get out of their houses, enter the workforce, and take on the world—was inspired in part by her own mother's experience.

When Friedan died in February 2006, Margalit Fox wrote this in a *New York Times* obituary: "[Friedan's] gifted, imperious mother, Miriam, had been the editor of the women's page of the local newspaper before giving up her job for marriage and children. Only years later while she was writing *The Feminine Mystique* did Ms. Friedan come to see her mother's cold, critical demeanor as masking a deep bitterness at giving up the work she loved."

And now, the latest defender of the stay-at-home mom, Caitlin Flanagan, writes in her book, *To Hell with All That: Loving and Loathing Our Inner Housewife*, about her feeling of abandonment when her mother's pronouncement "to hell with housework" resulted in her going back to work as a nurse. "On my first day as a latchkey child, I lost the key. A key was hidden under a stone for me, but I used it once and forgot to return it. It vanished immediately. Frustrated, my mother tied a third key on a piece of thick white string and hung it around my neck, a weighty reminder that I'd been dumped by Mom."

> "On my first day as a latchkey child, I lost the key. A key was hidden under a stone for me, but I used it once and forgot to return it. It vanished immediately. Frustrated, my mother tied a third key on a piece of thick white string and hung it around my neck, a weighty reminder that I'd been dumped by Mom."
> —Caitlin Flanagan

One might say that despite the intellectual underpinnings of their drastically different mandates to women, Friedan was scared into work by a bitter mother and Flanagan, who writes that she still feels anxious being alone in a house, was scarred forever by a mom who worked.

Most of the mothers in my survey felt, if not bound

by their own mothers' expectations, at least influenced by the kinds of mothers they were and the lives that they led. Comments like these, which revealed mother-daughter acceptance of each other, were frequent:

From a stay-at-home mom of two: "My mom worked when we kids were older. I think that's a good role model, especially for girls. I learned to cook and the whole family was happier because dinner was on time. Of course, she approves of my staying home now [while my kids are young]."

From a full-time career mother of two teenagers: "My mom was and is a role model to me. She always encouraged me, praised me, had great energy, and was physically and emotionally available to me. All of those qualities are things I'm trying to emulate as a mom."

From a working-outside-the-home mother of two young children: "My mom would make any kind of sacrifice for me, even though she was a single mom for a while, worked two jobs, and went to school. My mom would drop everything for me. I do the same for my children."

Also frequent were the more ambivalent comments revealing undertones of conditional approval:

From a full-time career mother: "My mom tells me, 'You need to do what you want to do,' but underneath she is critical of my job orientation. When I remarked to her that I would not be as good a full-time caretaker of our kids as our nanny is, she replied sharply, 'You would too! You'd be different, but you'd be just as good.' Then she suggested that the reason our child 'doesn't play well independently' is that the nanny is there all the time."

From another mom, who expressed the desire to be somewhat different from her own mom "[My mother] offered unconditional love, but wasn't as strong or emotionally mature as a child needs a parent to be. She was overly critical and sometimes played favorites, but was also caring and thoughtful."

Then there is the yearning of some modern moms to capture both the home-oriented world their moms provided and the career oriented world they themselves are pursuing. As one career mom wrote in her questionnaire:

> I wish I could do all the fantastic things my [stay-at-home] mom did, but I can't 'cause there is no way to make time! I think as a working mother, I have more concentrated time with my children. I try to make the best of that time and 'pack it all in' … but I also catch myself longing for the mundane daily activities with the kids too … I feel that I have another dimension to my life that my mom didn't have 'til much later … I do look back on my childhood very fondly and loved knowing my mom was always literally there. I'm not sure how things would have been different if she would have worked. …

Would it have been different?
Would *I* have been different?
How will my *kids* be different?
HOW WILL MY KIDS TURN OUT?

Those are the crux questions, especially for moms carving a new role, different from that of their mothers.

We moms are still assigned the major responsibility, by ourselves and by others, for raising "good kids," and that can color everything we do. Fathers have been severely criticized if they are absent or if they are abusive. Any negative action in between these two extremes is usually tolerated, forgiven, or viewed as peripheral.

And the advice to women over the decades on how to

"raise those kids" has been as frequent and varied as that on how to "lose those pounds!" Way back in 1946, the supposedly liberal and permissive Dr. Benjamin Spock wrote a special section in his first edition of *The Common Sense Book of Baby and Child Care* for those mothers who "have to work," thus showing his bias that they shouldn't. Now, some modern feminists advise that the only way to teach the value of work, especially to daughters, is to work yourself. In short, the sheer plethora of advice to moms is mind-boggling.

Then there are the pronouncements of one's peers, which can flame into a mini-war in a second, some more subtle than the stomach stab suffered by Jenn Watts, but still ...

Our daughter, Heather, while pregnant with her second boy and working full-time at her executive-level position, had lunch with a group of women, most of whom were staying home with small children or working part-time.

"Heather," said one, "I just don't know how you do it!"

"I don't know how I could not do it," she answered. (Her eyes flash with intensity even in the retelling.) "I simply must have that kind of challenge." Whereupon the subject quickly changed.

Then there are those thinly veiled questions asked by career mothers of at-home mothers. Witness this dialogue described by Renate Robey, retired journalist and stay-at-home mother of two:

Former colleague: "You're staying home full-time?"
Renate: "Yes." (With no explanation.)
Former colleague: "With no plans to go back?"
Renate: "No." (With no elaboration.)

"If I look them straight in the eye and don't defend or make excuses for my choice, that stops 'em cold!" she says with a laugh. She adds, however, that it took her about two years (she's been home six) to stop justifying herself with,

"But I'm happy to be home right now. I'll go back someday, and so forth, and so forth. ... "

The fact that it took this sophisticated forty-four-year old woman two years to stop justifying her choices to her contemporaries shows the power of the mommy mandates.

Yes, the mommy wars exist because moms have been determined the determiner. If her child becomes an ax murderer or a psychopath, it's mom's fault. If he or she wins the Nobel Prize, it's at least partly mom's doing, though credit doesn't come as quickly as blame.

And the mommy wars exist because the very connectivity of women to our mothers and other women—which, in its positive mode, is one of the reasons we live longer and seem to survive crises more easily than men—renders us supersensitive to the views of our sisters.

The early feminists proclaimed that such competitive phenomena as the mommy wars foul up our female psyches because the patriarchy set up women to fight over such things as mates, clothing, and social status. Meanwhile, the men could simply continue to scoop up the goodies—education, jobs, and so forth—while women fought among themselves.

I agree, but that should have been *yesterday*.

Today the mommy wars linger in part because the media and its pundits not only keep these wars on the front burners, but they also fan the flames of the stewing pots and zero in on these simmering sensitivities like a heat-seeking missile, assuming that the whole world loves a catfight.

And it does!

Take note of James Wolcott's literary depiction of mommies defending their respective turfs in the October 2, 2006, *New Republic*. In the article, titled "Meow Mix," he writes,

> Fierce tribes of Working Moms and Stay-at-Home Moms go at it on the soccer field, tufts of grass and tufts of hair flying from tornado clouds of swirling limbs. Armed with virtuous pride and bionic eyes that can spot every moral defect and child-rearing error across a crowded playground, the Working Mother and the Stay-at-Home Mother are convinced that the other is shortchanging herself and the future of her children—letting down the team, not to mention the nation.

So is this guy describing the wars or inciting them? And don't we female pundits also fan the flames? Take for example Caitlin Flanagan, author and stay-at-home mother of twin boys. Pulling on our maternal heartstrings, she lauds the women who have given up or bypassed careers: Unlike the working mothers, "a precision team" who arrived at the soccer game right on time, "click-clacked to their seats and fished tiny video cameras out of enormous purses," the "at-home mothers who had arrived early and ... were chatting expansively with each other. Many of them had toddlers in tow." She exults, "Why shouldn't they make a day of it? Having time to be fully present for their children is exactly why most of them don't work."

And as for the children of the stay-at-home moms, Flanagan writes that they will receive that blessing of "the sweetness of being with the person who loved them most in the world ... an immersion in the most powerful force on earth: mother love." So only noncareer mothers can provide that mother love immersion? Please!

But then there is Linda R. Hirshman beating up on the stay-at-home mom—especially the highly educated mom—in her book, *Get to Work: A Manifesto for Women of the World*: "Bounding home [dropping out of the workforce] is not good for women and it's not good for the society. The women aren't using their capacities fully; ... Whether they leave the workplace altogether or just cut back their commitment, their talent and education are lost from the public world to the private world of laundry and kissing boo-boos."

Each of these women might have some valid sociological as well as personal points. The way they prove their arguments, however, with heaps of denigration and guilt, certainly doesn't get us any closer to enlightenment.

But back to the kinder, gentler world that does exist. Despite the stomach stab delivered to Jenn Watts, there are times that the exclamation from a homemaker to a career woman—"I don't see how you do it!"—denotes real respect and support. And as the Reverend Regina Groff, who had earlier stayed home full-time herself, said in admiration of her stay-at-home sisters, "The stay-at-home mom has it the hardest [because]

> "My husband wouldn't let me work, and I might have been a better mom if I had."

sometimes the husband who is out in the workplace often does not see his wife's work as real work, when it is actually harder work!"

And let's face it—whatever mom situation one is in right now, it could change by next year or even next month. In much the same way that Regina Groff left full-time infant care to take on the caring and inspiring of a whole congregation, Stephanie Bender quit a job she loved to stay home with her two—soon to be three—children.

Just before *Daddy On Board* went to press, in the locker room of my workout club I heard a young mom tell a much older one that she might go back to work, really wanted to, but wasn't sure. The older mom replied, "Do it! My husband wouldn't let me work, and I might have been a better mom if I had." So there it is: from no choice to many choices to what choice do I make?

Most moms harbor real ambivalence about their choices even if not burdened by guilt. So when we challenge another mom, are we actually fighting the other side of ourselves? On bad days at work or at home, does the grass on the other side momentarily look greener? And to fight our attraction to a lusher pasture, do we dig our heels into our own turf even harder?

Echoing Miriam Peskowitz's Greek chorus of guilt in chapter two, James Wolcott writes, "Whatever choice a woman makes, or has foisted upon her by necessity and circumstance, ambivalence digs in its spikes. Women—to generalize madly—internalize a far thornier thicket of conflicts and tensions than most men do." He's right, but at the beginning of twenty-first-century America, can't we grow out of some of this ambivalence or at least recognize it as a psychic reality of our lives and move on?

As a young mom wrote on www.clubmom.com, June 20, 2006: "Basically, I just want us to remember to respect each other. That's my biggest issue with the so-called 'mommy wars'—that we damage ourselves most by not respecting each other."

Or as syndicated columnist Froma Harrop sums up: "Most women know they are giving up something to follow their current path [whatever it is]. They certainly don't deserve the harsh critiques of their juggling acts, whether coming from the outside or within."

Chapter Five
All Is Not Perfect in Parent Land

First there were eleven—couples, that is. But one interview never took place.

As I approached the family's suburban home on a brisk day in late fall, I heard loud accusations and recriminations coming through the open window. The words were unclear, but the tone was not. This was no kiddie battle, but a full-fledged adult fight.

The mom, whom I had met only once before, came out tearful and apologetic. "Sorry, but would you watch the kids in the yard for a while while we work this out?"

Of course.

Later, the mom, an executive-level career woman with two preschool-aged children, told me that her husband was fed up with her being "all job and kids," that she had no time for him. "And you know, he's right," she added. "I am trying to help him see that this is the most tense and pressured time I've ever had at work; I'm in the middle of a huge negotiation with incredible travel and I hate leaving the kids. I'm trying to explain that this will be over soon, that right now I just need to focus. ... "

Up until this point, my conversations with the couples have only alluded to some of the difficulties they face. To be sure, many of their problems and daily annoyances are shared by other parents, but how they solve the problems or address the annoyances can vary greatly.

Couple's Time

A uniform complaint from more than this one pair of parents was that the busyness of their lives left no alone time just to themselves, as couples.

Attorney Jon Bender put it poignantly in his questionnaire. "I miss the times when I had Stephanie [a stay-at-home mom of three] all to myself. Our relationship has taken a backseat to our child-raising efforts."

Both expressed in the interview that they wish they had had more time to be DINKs—dual income, no kids. "Actually we never did fit this acronym," Jon adds with a laugh. "When we were first married with no kids, we were both in grad school and had no income either!"

The Benders do take an occasional night out for a movie or dinner, but never both at once, as that would cost over $100 with a babysitter. "We sometimes try to have date nights at home after the kids are in bed," Stephanie adds wistfully.

Professor Robin Koenigsberg and Environmental Defense Director Dan Grossman express similar frustrations. "Political functions—when Dan was in the legislature—used to be our date nights, but now we don't have to do them, so we don't," said Robin.

They did "buy a babysitter" at a benefit for their children's preschool, "to force us to go out," adds Dan. Like the Benders, they have found that a full night out with a sitter costs more than $100, a luxury on top of the payments for their new home that they can seldom afford.

Medical resident Jenn Watts and realtor Dave Leuthold said in their November interview that they had taken very little time together, just the two of them, since July. They do take time with friends who have kids, but otherwise, says Dave, "We are just so cooked by the time the kids are down, it's too hard to arrange."

Karen and Paul LeFever say they do find more time

together now that they have teenagers, but to grab that time when the kids are little takes a lot of planning and prioritizing.

A longtime woman friend with four grown, married kids cautioned me in the preparation for my interviews for this book to watch for the red flag of no couple's time. "No time together can erode a marriage more than anything else," she said.

Sometimes it *is* a parent of a couple who will weigh in on this danger. It was public affairs consultant Eric Anderson's mom who spotted his and wife Renate Robey's potential red flag. "You guys have *got* to get out more," she said to the couple after they had spent a full year staying home and closely watching their second child, who was a preemie with birth complications.

"She's the most frugal person in the world," says Renate of her mother-in-law, "but she was right!" Now they hire a sitter and take every other Thursday evening as date night, no matter what.

Upon the original advice of Mom, they now value it, so they do it.

Money and Values

The couples in this study are in no way poor, but they are often stretched financially. A psychologist friend commented that money for them will often be a values issue, not a financial one. For these lucky people, it's not a choice of feeding the kids or turning up the heat. Still, money is always somewhat of an issue for most couples.

In our long marriage, Dick and I have always been in sync about the *big* money things. Do we really need a new car? No. Can we afford this trip this year? Yes. Are those Christmas gifts for the kids more than we can afford and more than they should expect? Probably. Let's scale back.

Yet one time when he questioned my need of a once-a-week cleaning service, I went ballistic! "Tell me how much cleaning *you* are willing to do," I remember yelling. "You clearly don't value my time!"

But then, I often didn't value his time—how much his daily earnings (even when I was working full steam and for full pay too) were what enabled our lifestyle and our secure retirement.

Money and values issues run through most of the lives of the parents featured in this book.

Robin Koenigsberg and Dan Grossman value public service, but they value time with their kids more, so he forgoes pursuing politics and takes a job with more pay and fewer hours. She could take a corporate job with a big pay increase that would probably allow him to stay in politics, but then, when would either of them see the kids?

Rob Carmody and Kim Ashley Carmody value the diversity of their neighborhood, the home they have redone themselves, and the close proximity of the house to both of their jobs. But it would cost less to have a bigger house, replete with a huge basement for Rob's hobbies, in the safer suburbs, with better schools. Looks like they will stay put for now, but later? And Kim, the primary wage earner, sometimes wonders what it would be like not to have to work.

Will Jenn Watts, after years of training, really take a part-time physician's job, forgo the bigger salary, even with loans to pay back, in order to spend more time with the children, especially if she and her husband decide to have a third baby? Will Dave then value her time at home, or wish she would make all the money she is capable of? And when he spends more time at the office, which he says he can do and wants to do when Jenn is done with her residency, will he miss the hours he has spent as prime caretaker of the children?

Sandra Donnell, a self-described nonspender from a nonspending family, tolerates with a laugh full-time stay-at-home dad Kent's wish to indulge in more toys for his own projects. But if she continues as the sole wage earner, will his wish to spend become more of a bone of contention than if he were earning a wage also? Will his own needs, along with his occasional feelings of isolation, propel Kent back to the workforce?

In our culture, and thus in our marriages, money can equal power, whether we want it to or not. At least two of the dual-income moms said to me that they just "had to" earn some of the family money, whether or not it was financially necessary.

> In our culture, and thus in our marriages, money can equal power, whether we want it to or not.

In my marriage I have felt the same way. At the times when I was not earning, I felt I had less power in decision making, even though I knew that such thinking was old fashioned and just plain stupid. Yet feeling powerless made me act powerless.

Conversely, Stephanie Bender, a full-time homemaker who manages all the family finances, felt she had too much of the power. She wrote on her questionnaire, "I just got sick of being the bad guy, always saying no to spending, so we figured out ways that Jon can be more involved in the money management of the house."

Corporate and personal coach Leslie Hilton advises that nothing can be of greater use than jointly working out a financial plan. I agree, especially because it gives a couple a concrete way to talk about priorities and values.

Psychotherapist and coach Laurie Weiss says that, unlike these couples whose values differ only at the margin, when individual members of a couple have truly different core values, trouble will eventually erupt, and often it will first surface over money.

She speaks of a mom who worked an executive-level job that involved long hours and much travel—she was often gone a week at a time. The dad worked at a lower-level job and assumed full responsibility for the children and household during the week. All was fine until mom, too, wanted to be home with the kids and decided to start her own business. He objected to her leaving her high-paying job, constantly belittled her and her ability to be successful, and found a mistress. They divorced because she wouldn't stay with him and allow him to have a mistress too.

Another man in another marriage I recently heard of truly values money above all. He and his wife work the same hours, but he makes twice as much money. Therefore, he says, she should do all the child care of their one daughter and all the housework. She is resentful, and they are in counseling.

But let's move on to how the couples interviewed for this book, all of whom seem to share core values, have negotiated or not negotiated their differences up to now, whether financial or otherwise.

Communication, or "I Can't Read Your Mind!"

Regina Groff says she and Peter used to argue about who does what, especially when she was at home full-time with the babies. "It was like we were always trying to prove who does more. ... And when we weren't arguing, I was full of bottled-up resentment."

"You were?" Peter interjects with a feigned look of incredulity. Regina rolls her eyes and continues, "Peter finally told me in exasperation, 'I can't read your mind, say what you need,' so I began to do just that, and it was a real turning point."

Stephanie Bender tells a similar story with a specific example. Realizing that earlier in our interview she had made Jon sound like a saint who just got it from the get-go, she elaborates. Still working after their first child was born, Jon, Stephanie says, had no idea how much energy it took just to get Teddy packed up and out of the house to go to his mother's for the day. "There I was rushing around, and he just didn't see it."

When she pointed this out in frustration, he simply took over all the "stuff preparation" every morning so that she could concentrate on the baby. "It was like, 'Oh, why didn't you say so?'" And what does Jon need? "We have talked about how it is hard for me to be home at a certain time every night. Stephanie now understands that I make every effort to get home as soon as I can.'"

Both my daughter, Heather, an executive with MediaNews Group, and my goddaughter, Annie Richardson, a nurse-midwife, have commented that "men just don't see it"—whatever it is that needs to be done. To that, we mothers, Lynette Richardson and I, best friends since 1959, shake our heads and say, "What do you expect? He can't read your mind!" Then we marvel in private at all their young husbands do and comment that we should have been so lucky. Later, we recall with some humor the saying of a mutual friend's grandmother: "Men are like wheelbarrows—they're useful, but you have to pick them up and dump them where they're needed." Perhaps not fair, but ...

Psychotherapist Laurie Weiss says that she hates to put the burden on women, but that the better communicator a wife is, the more her husband will learn by example and the better off the marriage will be.

Lisa Merlino, deputy director of Invest in Kids, often takes this communication initiative. "I'm such a processor," she writes. "We may feel differently about how to handle certain things ... [but] we'll always walk through things until we get to a good place."

> Psychotherapist Laurie Weiss says that she hates to put the burden on women, but that the better communicator a wife is the more her husband will learn by example and the better off the marriage will be.

A couple we know who are in the seventeenth year of their marriage, the second for each, found that writing down expectations often beats talking. During clerical counseling before their marriage, they were at first insulted and annoyed that the minister insisted they each make two lists: one was titled "What do I expect from my partner?" and the other was "What do I think my partner expects of me?" The items on each were to be in order of importance.

"Respect" was at the top of the wife's first list, as she had been psychologically abused in her first marriage. "Accepting my children" topped the husband's list, as he was a widower with a boy and a girl, both still of tender ages. Yet the couple found that the importance of the lists was not the content but the conversation process it initiated. "We use them to this day!" she exclaimed. "And it's never too late to start a list and then discuss the significance of each item and why it matters."

Psychiatrist and author David Viscott, in his classic 1974 book *How to Live With Another Person*, wrote, "It is sometimes helpful for two partners to correspond by mail over their disagreements, especially when a particular conflict is so painful that any discussion may lead to arguments that are unproductive and only worsen things."

A couple with three preschoolers, not in the study, has brought this advice into the new century with modern technology. "We always begin our negotiations with e-mail," she says. "That way we don't get off on the wrong foot with negative body language or tone." And avoiding such nonverbal messages are a constant challenge.

As one mom in the study said to me, "I finally learned not to burst out with blaming comments like 'You're not being fair!' but simple statements, in a calm voice, like 'I really need some time off.'"

Private Time

Jeff D. Opdyke, "Love & Money" columnist for *The Wall Street Journal*, wrote recently of his and his wife Amy's inability to find educational or creative time for themselves.

As the father of two children, ages ten and four, Opdyke discovered himself yearning to take Chinese lessons. "A language school stood just outside the doors of my train station. And each evening for more than a year, I told myself as I walked past that I was going to enroll in Mandarin classes. I figured I could pop in once a week, on my way to my car from the train. ... Alas, the only Chinese I picked up came off the back of the fortunes at Chinese restaurants." In short, although the cost of the lessons was well within the family budget, he found he just couldn't justify the money or the time.

Time alone for renewal is a reoccurring theme in my interviews, and a commonly yearned-for luxury.

Jon Bender says, "I wish I could continue guitar lessons and have more ski days with less guilt." Wife Stephanie adds, "And I'd like to read a book all the way through instead of five pages before I fall asleep. I'd like to take knitting lessons."

Lack of time for exercise, meditation, and wellness activities is a big loss for many. Yet finding the time for physical conditioning or nurturing of one's own body is far more common among the dads; at least four in the study are regular joggers. But three of the moms said that their own lack of exercise time was due much more to their internal conflicts than to conflicts with their spouse.

Jenn Watts says that when Dave comes home from work first, he will keep the nanny on for an extra hour and go for a jog. Whereas if she gets home first, she will let the nanny go immediately and "spend every minute with the kids." Both she and Stephanie Bender have rejoined health clubs in order to "make themselves" go, but each admits it doesn't always work.

Robin Koenigsberg's yoga has "completely fallen out. I will always get one more thing done instead of going. I'm not willing to trade off my time with the kids or my sleep!"

Lisa Merlino's political consultant husband, Jim, whose schedule is more flexible, has exercise built into his day, but for her it has "completely dropped off the program." Yet some of the moms do exercise with baby in the jogging stroller.

Renate Robey has found a way to be alone even when she is not alone. When the kids are playing or asleep, she listens to books on tape while she does the housework.

> "The biggest sacrifice of parenthood is giving up unstructured time."
> —Eric Anderson

Another mother of three, not in my sample, says she has trained her small children to treat "Mommy's bath time" as uninterruptible alone time. She starts the bubbles, takes a book, and soaks and reads for an hour. Of course, in both of these examples, one ear is always tuned in to kids' pleas, noises, ultraquietness, or other hints of potential trouble. And for some, this speck of alertness does not allow the real mental alone time needed.

As Eric Anderson writes, "The biggest sacrifice of parenthood is giving up unstructured time. I used to love to just lounge around reading, listening to music, staring at the ceiling. I've found that young kids demand constant attention from the predawn moment my son would wake me with a poke in the ribs and 'Daddy, let's play' to the bedtime routine. I find parenthood—especially when the kids were young—unrelenting and exhausting."

How well I remember!

When my kids were still preschoolers and I came home from a political meeting or shopping trip, I recall sneaking into our master bedroom through a patio door and taking a half hour for myself before I greeted the children and released the babysitter. At first they were amazed to see Mommy emerging from the bedroom, but pretty soon they caught on and instinctively seemed to know when to start banging on the door.

Another woman, a writer and mom of two preschool-ers (and the only part-time work-from-home mom I talked to), laughs as she tells me by phone that she would rather "go pee in the bushes" than come back into her house from her backyard

> Parents who value each other and pour time and resources into their children may have learned to be *too* selfless.

office when her children are there with her husband or the nanny; it's so important that she have alone time to work and concentrate, that she won't interrupt it even for her own minor emergencies.

Couples seem to find it harder to pay a babysitter for alone time than for couple's time. Again, it is a matter not only of what is affordable, but what is most valued. And parents who value each other and pour time and resources into their children may have learned to be *too* selfless.

Genuine encouragement from one's spouse can help justify the time or expense, though such support is no guarantee. Columnist Opdyke, who is now trying to per-suade his wife, Amy, to take painting lessons, writes, "I think she'd benefit from that more than I'd benefit from Chinese lessons at the moment, and someone has to stick around to watch over the kids. But she doesn't know if she has the time just yet."

Perhaps alone time needs should be budgeted, sched-uled, written down, then discussed, just like financial needs.

Flash Points, or "You Don't Respect My Time!"

Jennifer Watts writes on her questionnaire, "One Saturday I asked David to stay with the girls while I went out to do one quick errand. When I was out, many more things dawned on me that I wanted to do, and I was out for more than three hours. David was angry and said that I act like I don't value his time, and that I value mine more." She adds that, although compromise and respecting the other's time and need to be away is "an ethic they both try to uphold," she doesn't feel they're able to truly resolve these issues while she is a resident. "We live very day to day now."

Robin Koenigsberg mentions how the natural tensions of work and kids explode, especially when there is "no one around to blame but each other." Her wits will go in the morning when she's trying to get the kids ready to drop off at daycare or preschool on her way to work. "Sometimes, I just lose it and yell and scream." Dan, on the other hand, is more likely to go quiet, especially at night when the baby is fussy and it's his turn. "I'll just sulk." How long? "Sometimes twenty-four hours," he adds sheepishly.

Rob Carmody, who wrote so eloquently about the unexpected joys of becoming a dad and his commitment to paternity leave, also writes of the stresses that pulled on them when he was on family leave and Kim was working from home: "I was doing a fair amount of contract work to supplement our income and that limited my time spent with Mackenzie [their younger daughter]. [Then] to get other projects done around the house—it kept me from getting into a regular routine. Kim and I were constantly butting heads with each other since we were always around each other."

These two examples, along with others from different couples, exhibit the struggles and challenges of the nuclear family. Yes, each little unit is a nurturing place that can raise nurtured children to mature adulthood, but where do the tensions fly? Robin's comment that there is "no one around to blame but each other" rings true. All admit that pure exhaustion can ignite their flash points at any time. The ones who had extended family—usually parents—in town who would come in at crisis points were grateful for this support and release.

Lisa Merlino doesn't know what she would have done if her mom had not come one night to relieve her when work, kids, and political tension went sky-high and political consultant Jim could not be home.

Working parents Kent Gardener and Sandra Donnell will be forever thankful for her mom, who came from out of state at the end of Sandra's pregnancy when Kent was finishing up a huge contracting job.

Regina and Peter Groff mentioned more than once the support of his parents and sister as well as her mother and stepfather, who moved to Denver to be near Regina, their only child, and their grandchildren. On the Thursday nights during the legislative session that Regina has church meetings, Regina's folks, who live right across the street, take over until Peter comes home.

But many couples with children do not have parents or other family close and often must rely solely on their own wits. Stay-at-home dad Paul LeFever and his wage-earning wife, Karen, whose kids are now teens and who "have been in the parenting business a long time," say that when they are exhausted they just defuse the flash points until morning. Contrary to the old adage "Never go to bed angry," Paul emphasizes that after a decent, if not long, sleep, things look different and will be more solvable in the morning. Perhaps, but …

Three dads speak humorously but pointedly about what mornings can bring. Peter Groff writes, "Mornings are the hardest time for me because it is usually my job to get the kids off and my son ALWAYS takes his time." Another father of two young ones, the husband of the writer with the backyard office, writes of the tension that builds up at breakfast time over "the excruciatingly complex negotiation related to getting the food into the child's mouth." And a third one told the most dramatic story: On a cold winter's day he had painstakingly helped his three-year-old get dressed for preschool. It seemed to take ages. Then, in the one minute he took to go get their coats, his son had taken off every stitch of clothing and piled it neatly on the floor beside him.

It's 7:30 A.M. and just as I write this, an e-mail pops up from my daughter-in-law, Cindy. Actually, it is from my son, Scott, writing cryptically on his wife's account that he is answering for her because Kennon—their six-month-old—is fussing like crazy, and she's trying to get out the door to work, and he's trying to help, and. ...

Clearly there is no perfect time to air the gripes and diffuse the tension.

Negotiation and Triage

Robin Koenigsberg writes this answer to a question regarding how couples negotiate and work out issues: "It often feels more like triage. The distribution of duties needs to change daily, based on our work schedules and other demands on our time. At any given time, one of us may be feeling like we're carrying the lion's share. ... We often end up tallying up what we've done for the children for the day to convince the other that we're pulling our share. Rather than negotiating, we've gotten pretty good at reading the signs and recognizing when the other is just venting or is really over the top maxed out and in need of a break. But sometimes we miss the signs."

> "We often end up tallying up what we've done for the children for the day to convince the other that we're pulling our share. Rather than negotiating, we've gotten pretty good at reading the signs and recognizing when the other is just venting or is really over the top maxed out and in need of a break."
>
> —Robin Koenigsberg

And sometimes the signs can be misinterpreted. Roger Fisher, William Ury, and Bruce Patton, in their classic negotiation book *Getting to Yes*, suggest that something taken as in insult, like Jenn staying out shopping for three hours, is not necessarily meant that way. Yet it would be very easy for Dave, perhaps already feeling besieged, to assume that she does not value him or their relationship when she actually may have been getting extra things done early so she wouldn't have to ask him to do them later. But he won't know that if she doesn't tell him. And this is best done in a nondefenisve, straightforward manner. According to Fisher, Ury, and Patton, whether it's a couple's argument or a business impasse, intentions should be clarified and the tendency to jump to a conclusion put on hold.

One young couple not in the survey say they negotiate everything and will usually reach a truce, but, adds the dad, "especially when the argument is about whose turn it is to sleep, it's not so pretty getting there."

Paul and Karen LeFever have found a way to keep negotiations from becoming too off the wall. After twenty-one years of marriage, they have become pretty good at "stepping away from a debate or disagreement—without walking away. There *is* a difference," they maintain. "Stepping away is okay—walking away is not. It is hard to explain the difference, but we both know when we are doing it to postpone negotiation versus just walking away angry."

Jon and Stephanie Bender have found that their flash points are most likely to flare up around their children's negative behavior, so they have negotiated an original solution that keeps heated situations from getting out of control—especially when the kids are involved. Stephanie says:

> Our oldest son played soccer last fall. Each time we arrived
> for a game, he would become clingy and weepy and have a
> lot of anxiety about playing. This was incredibly frustrat-
> ing for both of us. Jon would really lose his cool and I
> would chastise him for doing so; this in turn would lead to
> a fight. The [three] kids, of course, would sense our tension
> and the whole thing would get worse and worse.
>
> Since that time, we have decided that we have to take

turns. One of us needs to have a calming influence when the other is upset, frustrated, or stressed. Sometimes we are even explicit, saying, for example, "It's my turn to be stressed out about this right now." [The stress] can be about the kids, our financial situation, how messy the house is—anything.

I'm intrigued that this solution flies in the face of another old adage: "As parents, always be consistent in front of your kids." Yet for Jon and Stephanie, the turn-taking seems to work, and in many ways it is more emotionally honest: "Dad's mad and that's okay. I'm here." Or, "Mom's mad and that's okay. I'm steady."

In the same manner, Paul and Karen LeFever don't let rigid consistency get in their way when it comes to discipline; they agree to disagree. Paul, who will never use physical punishment, says they have agreed that whichever parent is "on the job" gets to discipline the way he or she sees fit.

He Helps, but I'm Responsible!

Other role-sharing flash points may arise when a career mother feels that no matter how much her husband does, she is still in charge of the day-to-day house and kid management. As one says, "I do the research on everything that the kids do, school activities, [and so forth]. I tend to be the one who makes sure that the details are taken care of, like buying birthday presents, school snacks. ... I'm always trying to hammer out the logistics of the day and the month."

Or as another mom puts it, "I sometimes feel resentful of the fixed responsibilities of cooking and grocery shopping and making sure the kids have everything they need: diapers, school supplies, food, milk. It feels like I've gotten stuck with many of the traditional female household jobs."

Complicating these resentments is the fact that the moms can feel guilty about them. "Am I just complaining," asks one, "when my husband already does so much?"

Linda Hirshman, in *Get to Work: A Manifesto for Women of the World*, writes, "Even when working [outside the home], women in the heterosexual, two parent family do 70 percent of the household labor. Maybe it is a natural compulsion." Although most of the dads in my survey appear to pull a bigger load than 30 percent, if one counts the planning and arranging hours, perhaps the working mom still does close to 70 percent.

But note Hirshman's last sentence, "Maybe it is a natural compulsion." So, is it partly *our* job as females to reduce that "natural" compulsion? I remember a mom from my era who tried to turn over some of the house and child management to her husband, but "he just didn't do it the right way."

Not the right way, or just not her way?

Something I've tried to keep in mind since then is that his way may be okay and that if I really want it done perfectly my way, I'd better do it myself. We say we want to let go of the management jobs, but if it means giving up control, we sometimes won't let it happen, thus sabotaging ourselves.

Interesting, but perhaps not surprising, is that no stay-at-home parent, male or female, voiced resentment about being constantly in charge. Although

> If I really want it done perfectly my way, I'd better do it myself.

they listed many of the management jobs as their responsibilities, it is as if in staying home, the household and schedule management is part of the understood deal.

Stay-at-home mom Renate Robey even uses some of the personal time she pays a babysitter for to get more things done so the weekend will be pressure-free and easier for the whole family.

Stay-at-home dad Paul LeFever does the cooking,

shopping, car and yard maintenance, and bill paying because he's good at those, although wife, Karen, takes care of the social schedule.

Lisa and Jim Merlino try not to get stuck in gender roles. As Lisa writes, "We have divided the chores between us—as a married couple and then again, as parents. There are times when I feel burdened by more because I'm quick to act when I see a need instead of asking for help." Yet Lisa adds that when either one of them identifies an imbalance, they discuss an appropriate solution that will work for both and will allow each to feel supported by the other.

Regina Groff notes at the end of her survey that she and Peter have kind of moved on. "We used to argue a lot about responsibilities. But once we began to honor each other's work and time equally, we began to compromise more. ... Basically we needed to get over ourselves and learn to appreciate each other."

Sex, Sensitivity, and Domestic Foreplay

A couple of weeks after my series of interviews, I received an e-mail from one of the moms.

"You asked us what we missed in our marriage since we had children," she wrote. "Well I forgot to tell you one thing—sex!"

Immediately I wrote her back and asked her if she would care to elaborate. No answer. Her revelation and her following silence made me realize that out of respect for my interviewees' privacy or due to my own reticence—probably both—I had not pushed them on this subject. So I went back over the individual questionnaires for information I might have missed.

> "You asked us what we missed in our marriage since we had children. Well I forgot to tell you one thing—sex!"

Their reluctance was striking. Clearly, I had made it easy for them to avoid the issue. The word *sexual* was only mentioned once, and in that case it was tucked away in the context of a larger question. Here is the question:

> Are you resentful of any of the roles you have taken on as a parent? Which ones? If so, do you think that this resentment affects the following in any significant wayo:
>
> (Please circle, and elaborate if you wish.)
> a) Self-esteem
> b) Marital communication
> c) Sexual desire or performance
> d) Performance at work
> e) The quality of your parenting
> f) Other

Of the ten couples interviewed, eight dads and nine moms sent in a completed questionnaire. Of these, five dads and six moms answered no to the first question listed above: "Are you resentful of any of the roles you have taken on as a parent?" although some of the same people did respond to the more specific portions of the questions that followed.

However, of the eight dads, only two answered that resentments over parenting roles affected their sexual desire or performance. Neither elaborated. The other six left the question blank.

Of the nine moms who answered the questionnaire, four reported that resentments over their roles affected their sexual desire or performance, four left the question blank, and one indicated that becoming a parent had made her sex life better. She writes, "With the exception of post-partum recovery, [sex] has only improved as we are more in love than ever after experiencing the miracle of bringing a child into this world."

Of the four women who circled "sexual desire or per-formance" as affected, only one elaborated, but she clarified that it wasn't really resentment, but the energy of child rearing itself. "I do think that the high level of output ... kills any sexual desire. It is hard for my husband to understand that sex is the thing that falls off my very full plate. I try to tell him that this is temporary."

Her obvious angst about this brought to mind a conversation I had with another mother (not in the study) with three superactive school-age kids. "I love my husband, I love sex," she said. "That is, when all the stars are aligned. "But I am the hub of so many wheels, I can't think of one more thing when the day is over. Sex, being asked to prepare a gourmet meal—*anything*—will put me over the top!"

> "I love my husband, I love sex. That is, when all the stars are aligned. But I am the hub of so many wheels, I can't think of one more thing when the day is over. Sex, being asked to prepare a gourmet meal—*anything*—will put me over the top!"

A young woman in my workout class expressed, breathlessly, between push-ups, that maybe she and her husband would not have that second child they'd planned because they were just too busy. When I asked if she meant that they were too busy to give the time to a second baby because of their demanding careers, she said, "No, we're just too busy to have sex."

The one mom in the survey who tells her husband that her lack of energy is only "temporary" brings to mind the mom at the beginning of this chapter who was too upset to be interviewed. To her husband's complaint that she had no time for him she said, "I try to tell him this [period of pressure at work] will be over soon."

Are men more insistent, then, that attention be paid, that sex be engaged in *now*, not later? Are women more likely to see life in waves or cycles, with the attitude that "this too will pass?" A gross generalization and a myth? Perhaps. Although experts in psychology have suggested that this male "impatience" is supported by biological and genetic research. Testosterone, in fact, is real!

The two men in my survey who circled the sex answer did not elaborate on *how* their desire or performance was affected, yet there were other places in the questionnaire where each had commented on life just being too hectic, too busy, or too frantic. If, like some of the moms, their plates were also too full to engage in sex,

> My interviewees were willing to admit a plethora of other failings, to poke fun at themselves, and be comfortable with their faults. But not about sex.

they probably would not have directly admitted it, especially if they saw such an admission as diminishing their masculinity.

The reluctance of both genders to respond to the sex question, when they had been effusive about so many other things, is perhaps a symptom of our culture's glorification of sex to the point where everyone is supposed to want it, revel in it, and excel in it, all the time.

My interviewees were willing to admit a plethora of other failings, to poke fun at themselves, and be comfortable with their faults. But not about sex. And, let's face it, even in this age of openness, for some, sex is simply too private to discuss.

God forbid that one would be seen as lacking in that area! We want to know all about it, but we don't want to talk about it, for fear of not measuring up.

I have also surmised from women of all ages that to complain about sex or lack of sexual desire might reflect badly on their husbands, even when they are really talking about themselves. So reticence could be translated as protectiveness.

Mine is not a statistical study, but a small trend did stand out. Of the four women who reported that resentments or their roles had affected their sexual drive or performance, three of these had also reported earlier in the survey that their main gripes in their marriage were not over parenting roles, but over the amount of or kinds of housework they did.

Although hard statistics are lacking on exactly what and how much housework is performed by moms as opposed to dads, Harvey Mansfield notes in his 2006 book, *Manliness*, that in a recent study, even though 90 percent of husbands and wives believe that caring for children and housework should be split 50-50, when that vacuum actually hits the carpet, women do two-thirds of it—which is close to Hirshman's earlier estimate of 70 percent.

The following correlation might seem like a stretch, but, incredible as it may sound, it has been verified by recent research. Author Neil Chethik, who reports on a national study of 300 husbands for his new book, *VoiceMale*, has found that "The happier a wife is with her husband's participation in housework, the more sex she has with him." As one of his interviewees, Joseph Fields, a thirty-nine-year-old guidance counselor, reports, "My wife has told me that she's never more turned on to me than when I'm doing housework. And she's proven it again and again." To paraphrase Chethik and the men he interviewed: Husbands—forget the bedroom for a bit; head for the kitchen! Dish washing is more romantic than chocolates or roses. Don't go for the jewelery and the music; go for the soap and the Brillo pads.

> Dish washing is more romantic than chocolates or roses.

What's going on here? It's clearly not just the housework. It's the appreciation that is revealed by a husband's pitching in, particularly in spontaneous and unexpected ways. It's the understanding of her load that the wife hears. It's that in the midst of their chaotic lives, their child-centered focus, he gets it and cares.

And appreciation breeds receptivity.

Late-breaking news: The long-reluctant correspondent—
the one who said one of the things
she and her husband missed since
having kids was sex—finally weighs in! Since her revela-
tions seem reflective of both the female and male sexual
state of mind, I include them in full.

"It's been seven days, honey."

> So the lack of desire is something my girlfriends and I
> joke about all the time. I would say this is a very common
> phenomenon after kids, mostly after adding the second for
> my husband and me. Personally, I think it comes down to
> two key reasons for us: lack of personal time and lack of
> sleep. Once you add a second child, all the personal time
> you had previously gets taken by child number two. For
> me, there's not much time to read, exercise, or do much of
> anything by myself or for myself. Most days the only alone,
> introspective time I get is the time between getting in bed
> and falling asleep. Add on top of that the reduction of sleep
> due to feedings, teething, and toddler bad dreams and the
> desire for a good night in bed just sleeping far outweighs
> any other kind of good night in bed.
>
> Now my husband, on the other hand, would forgo
> sleep any time for sex so he doesn't share these same feel-
> ings. Therefore, the tension it adds to our marriage is in
> the form of guilt. I feel so bad if it's been over a week that
> I'll resort to some sort of "okay let's have five minutes of
> lovin' before we go to sleep" type of sympathy sex. I think
> he understands somewhat that given the breast-feeding,
> high-stress job, and parenting, I prioritize sleep over sex
> right now and tries to be happy with whatever time we
> spend without too much pressure, comments, or pleading.
> Although I'm sure most days he wants to put up a huge
> sign that says "It's been seven days, honey."
>
> As for our role as parents, I think good, satisfied
> partners make good, satisfied parents. I can see that in

myself, on the rare night that my husband and I do have time to reconnect; the next morning I'm more affectionate with him, more relaxed with the kids, and overall more grounded. Luckily for us, we have good communication so it's something we discuss openly. It's definitely something that's taken a backseat for the last year, but we both know it's only temporary. For now, the occasional night of romance, a lingering pat, and catching each other's knowing look while tending to the kids gets us by.

Final Thoughts

Way back at the beginning of this book, I asked, "Have times really changed? Are younger, professionally educated dads actually changing diapers, serving up meals, and, more than that, feeling as responsible for what happens on the home front as moms always have?"

In most cases, at least in this study, the answer is a resounding yes! Dads are clearly on board the family boat, and even steering the ship—far more than they were in the sixties and seventies. I am still in absolute awe of the ways dads have changed, and I have to give them, and the moms to whom they are married, credit. For both are taking giant steps into unknown waters, sometimes with no role models for the new directions in which they sail.

> Tradition can tug like an undertow, and old ways die hard.

When my husband and I took even baby steps toward a dual-income marriage and coparenting, the fact that we were charting new waters made it very easy to misread the compass, to lose our direction and our footing, and to topple into the surf. Tradition can tug like an undertow, and old ways die hard.

I still don't have all the answers to parenting and role-sharing dilemmas, or marital grievances, and neither do the couples I interviewed—but that's the point. Each of these couples is using what works best for them to make decisions at this stage in their lives. They don't live by adages and conventional wisdom, but by being open when something just isn't working. They have found that unaired needs become resentments between partners—especially with women.

As career coach Leslie Hilton says, "In role sharing, everything is negotiable. Men often learn negotiation from the business world. In the home, if things are working well for them, they don't negotiate. Why should they? Women (even though they are generally better communicators) often don't know how to negotiate, or they accept traditional roles as givens even when they would like change. Thus, they accept that status quo, but seethe."

So if one adage does stand out, it is "Talk about it," in whatever style works for you; *negotiate* to agreement, even though "it's not so pretty getting there."

Marriage is hard. Parenting is hard. And acknowledging this without guilt or embarrassment for the choices you make is essential. Parenthood is a reward in itself.

I cannot close this chapter without putting in a few tips—and a bit of advice that comes from friends, family, and experience.

So, as a thriver and survivor in an almost forty-five-year marriage, as a member of a thirty-six-year women's support group, as the mother of two active toddlers who in a mini-second turned into two challenging teens, and as the proud grandmother of three "perfect" grandsons, here goes. ...

> Marriage is hard. Parenting is hard. And acknowledging this without guilt or embarrassment for the choices you make is essential. Parenthood is a reward in itself.

For wives: If you truly want household help, let go of perfection and control. One woman in the study mentioned "boy clean versus girl clean." Unless Dad is doing something life threatening (like not using soap to scrub the salmon skin off the cutting board) or limb threatening (like leaving that soapy water from the cutting board on the tile floor), boy clean is fine. Get used to it!

For husbands: Listen, then listen some more. Don't rush in and try to fix it. She may only want to be understood. As psychotherapist Laurie Weiss suggests, "It's only natural to want to help to solve a problem. ... Try asking, 'What can I do to help?'" She may then indicate if she wants a hand, or only an ear.

For both: Learn to apologize, even when it is not entirely your fault. This doesn't mean taking total blame, telling a lie, or becoming a martyr. "Hey, I really goofed up there," or "I'm really sorry for my part in that" can go a long way. Or as an elderly gent recently profiled in a regional newspaper quipped when asked what had led to the success of his sixty-year marriage, "Three little words, 'I was wrong.'"

Never use contempt in your communication, whether verbal or nonverbal. Turning your back, shaking your head in disgust, or walking away erodes a relationship more than anything else. It communicates a dismissal of his or her ideas or puts the person in a subordinate position. Contemptuous words or deeds are far more damaging than direct criticism.

Much as the couples in this study have done, learn to value your partner's interests as much as you value your own.

And ... in the words of the old Billy Joel song, "Tell her [or him] about it!" Give compliments. Say thanks. Express appreciation. Communication is more than saying what *you* need or what your spouse needs to do. When a grateful, warm, tender, or sexy thought pops into your mind, express it.

Laugh! There are few tensions a little humor can't ease. Life is fun.

Children are the most fun.
And those kids will grow up all too soon!

Appendix A
Letter to Participants

Dear [participant],

Thank you for agreeing to share your thoughts and experiences for my new book on how parenting roles have changed over the past forty years (with particular emphasis on the difference between the early 1970s and the beginning of the twenty-first century).

Attached is a questionnaire that I hope each of you as individuals will fill out and send back to me. After that, I will arrange a time of mutual convenience to interview you as a couple. Questions answered in the questionnaire will be treated as confidential, and no answers will be brought up in the interview unless a participant brings it up him-/herself. You need not answer every question.

Also, although my book may contain your thoughts and comments, no person or couple will be identified by name unless he/she/they give permission. (Neither will your ideas be shared with others in casual conversation.) I approach this subject with the confidentiality parameters of a social worker, as well as with the inquiring mind of a journalist.

As a finished product, I hope the book will be a resource to middle-class married parents of young children and also prod American institutions to better support these parents and the children they are raising.

Again, thank you for your time (which I know is scarce!) and your interest.

Dottie Lamm

Appendix B
Sample Questionnaire

Name:
Age:
Phone:
E-mail:

Section I
Years married:
Number of children:
Age and gender of children:
Education and degrees obtained:
Profession and job currently held:
    Full-time? (Hours per week_____)
    Part-time? (Hours per week_____)

What percentage of these hours are hours worked from home?

Section II
1.) If you work from home, do you find you can take care of your child/children simultaneously?
How do you make that work?

2.) Were you given, and did you take, maternity or paternity leave when your child was born or first adopted?

    a) How many weeks/months did you take?
    b) How much time was paid leave?
    c) How much was unpaid?

3.) Your personal approximate earnings per year—circle one category:
    a) Under $50,000
    b) $50,000–$100,000
    c) $100,000–$150,000
    d) $150,000–$200,000
    e) $200,000–$250,000
    f) Above $250,000

Section III

1.) Are you a full-time stay-at-home parent?

2.) Whether you are in the paid workforce or you are a full-time stay-at-home parent, how many hours per week do you estimate you spend on child rearing or child-related activities?

3.) Please list some examples of these activities in order of time spent, from the most time to the least time:

4.) Which of these activities do you most enjoy?

5.) Least enjoy?

6.) How many hours per week do you rely on alternate child care?

7.) What type of child care? Please circle:
    a) Day care center
    b) Day care home
    c) Your parents or other relative

d) Nanny
e) Part-time babysitter
f) Friend
g) Other

Section IV

1.) How have your and your spouse's time spent with the children or in child-related activities changed over the years?

2.) What are the reasons for any above changes?

3.) When you and your spouse disagree on who does what, how much, and when, do you negotiate to an agreement?

   How? Please give an example.

4.) Are there parenting role issues you and your spouse are still working out where answers and feelings might be unresolved?

   a) What are these issues?
   b) Do you feel you will be able to resolve these?
   c) If yes, how?
   d) If not, why not?

5.) Are you resentful of any of the roles you have taken on as a parent? Which ones?

6.) If so, do you think that this resentment affects the following in any significant ways: (Please circle, and elaborate if you wish.)
   a) Self-esteem
   b) Marital communication

    c) Sexual desire or performance
    d) Performance at work
    e) The quality of your parenting
    f) Other

7.) Is unpaid volunteerism your main career at this time?

8.) If so, do you think that the time and energy spent on it is as respected by yourself and your spouse as much as your paid work would be, or has been?

Section V

1.) How do you see your parenting role as differing from the parent of your same gender who parented you?

2.) Is this parent a role model, or someone you want to be different from, or both?
Please describe, and give examples where possible.

3.) Is your parent of the opposite gender a role model in any way? How?

4.) Did a grandparent, another relative, or a mentor influence the parenting roles you take on today? How?

Bibliography

Addeco, U.S.A. "Would Working Dads Take a Pass at Paternity Leave?" Press release announcing survey results, Melville, NY, June 4, 2007.

Blaffer Hrdy, Sara, and Mary Batten. "Daddy Dearest: What Science Tells Us About Fatherhood." *Time*, June 18, 2007.

Chethik, Neil. "Men and Housework: The Real Connection between Chores and Your Sex Life." iVillage.com, April 2007, http://love .ivillage.com/lnm/lnmgetcloser/0,,bg007hqj,00.html.

Cohany, Sharon R., and Emy Sok. "Trends in Labor Force Participation of Married Mothers of Infants." *Monthly Labor Review*, February, 2007.

Fisher, Roger, William Ury, and Bruce Patton. *Getting to Yes: Negotiating Agreement Without Giving In, 2nd ed.* Penguin: New York, 1991.

Flanagan, Caitlin. *To Hell with All That: Loving and Loathing Our Inner Housewife.* New York: Little, Brown and Company, 2006.

Fox, Margalit. "Betty Friedan, Who Ignited Cause in 'Feminine Mystique,' Dies at 85." *The New York Times*, February 5, 2006.

Goldberg, Carey. "Single Dads Wage Revolution, One Bedtime Story at a Time." *The New York Times*, June 17, 2001, sec. 1, 14.

Harrop, Froma. "Ladies' Closet of Anxieties," *The Denver Post*, June 8, 2007, 7B.

Hirshman, Linda R. *Get to Work: A Manifesto for Women of the World.* New York: Viking Penguin, 2006.

Jewett, Sarah Orne. *A Country Doctor.* Boston: Houghton-Mifflin, 1884.

Lewis, Al. "Full-Time Dads Worth Six Figures." *The Denver Post*, June 17, 2007, 1K.

Mansfield, Harvey. *Manliness*. New Haven, CT: Yale University Press, 2006.

Opdyke, Jeff D. "So Many Interests, So Little Time." *The Wall Street Journal*, July 15, 2007.

Peskowitz, Miriam. *The Truth Behind the Mommy Wars*, Emeryville, CA: Seal Press, 2005.

Rivers, Caryl, and Rosalind Barnett. "Gasp! I Married a Career Woman." WomensEnews.org, September 1, 2006.

Rochlen, Aaron. "U-Texas SAHF research results." DadStaysHome .com, April 4, 2007. www.dadstayshome.com/dads/showthread .php?t=5002.

Trillin, Calvin. *About Alice*. New York: Random House, 2006.

Turner, Jim. www.genuineblog.com.

U.S. Bureau of the Census. *Table SHP-1: Parents and Children in Stay-At-Home Parent Family Groups: 1994 to Present*. March 27, 2007, http://www.census.gov/population/socdemo/hh-fam/shp1.xls.

Viscott, David. *How to Live with Another Person*. New York: Pocket Books, 1974.

Wolcott, James. "Meow Mix." *The New Republic*, October 2, 2006.

www.salary.com. "Stay-at-Home Dad's Salary $128,755—Nearly $10,000 Less Than Stay-at-Home Mom's." Salary.com, June 13, 2007, http://salary.com/sitesearch/layoutscripts/sisl_display .asp?filename=&path=/destinationsearch/par662_body.html.

www.salary.com. "Mom Deserves a Raise in 2007: Working Mom and Stay-at-Home Mom Salaries For 2007." Salary.com, September, 2007, http://salary.com/sitesearch/layoutscripts/sisl_display .asp?filename=&path=/destinationsearch/personal/par642_body .html.

ZablitSun, Jocelyne. "Mr. Mom Becoming More of a Household Name in U.S." daddyfu.jelyou.com, April 8, 2007. http://daddyfu.jelyon .com/2007/04/.

About the Author

Dottie Lamm has been involved in the fight for women's equality and reproductive rights as first lady of Colorado, as a Colorado Democratic candidate for U.S. Senator, and

as a columnist for *The Denver Post*, among other positions. She earned her BA in psychology at Occidental College and her MSW at the University of Denver's Graduate School of Social Work. Lamm came to Colorado from California in 1959 as a United Airlines flight attendant. She met her husband, Dick Lamm, future governor of Colorado, in 1961 and they married in 1963. She is an active freelance writer and public speaker, serves on the Colorado Access Board, and enjoys spending time with her grandsons. A twenty-six-year survivor of breast cancer, she still skis, hikes, and bikes. She lives with her husband in Denver, Colorado.